Kick-start
Learning Russian:
2000 RUSSIAN Words You
didn't Know You Knew

LAWRENCE BURNS

MULTITRAIN Publishing

Disclaimer

The material in this publication is of the nature of general
comment only, and does not represent professional advice. It is
not intended to provide specific guidance for particular
circumstances and it should not be relied on as the basis for any
decision to take action or not take action on any matter which it
covers. Readers should obtain professional advice where
appropriate, before making any such decision. Therefore, if you
wish to apply ideas contained in this book, you are taking full
responsibility for your actions. To the maximum extent permitted
by law, the author and publisher disclaim all responsibility and
liability to any person, arising directly or indirectly from any person
taking or not taking action based upon the information in this
publication.

National Library of Australia Cataloguing-in-Publication entry:

Creator: Burns, Lawrence, 1956- author.
Title: Kick-start learning Russian: 2000 Russian words you didn't
know you knew / by Lawrence Burns.
Edition: First
ISBN: 9780994641601 (paperback)
Subjects: Russian language--Spoken Russian.
        Russian language--Compound words--Dictionaries.
        Russian language--Orthography and spelling--Dictionaries.
Dewey Number: 491.7152

ISBN-10: 0-9946416-0-5
ISBN-13: 978-0-9946416-0-1

DEDICATION

This book is dedicated with love to mothers Iris and Ninelia.
They taught me speak.

To the children Stephen, Alison, Ekaterina and Daria whom I
love equally and who always kept me on my toes.

Kick-start Learning Russian:
2000 RUSSIAN Words You didn't Know You Knew

CONTENTS

PREFACE

Languages have words which can be traced back to sources in other countries. Many languages borrow/ adopt words from each other. Some words are constructed from the classical ancient languages, such as Latin or Greek. Other words are borrowed from indigenous people. Most of these words can be called "international" because their versions are used in many European languages and often are cross-cultural. Despite the language people speak, all of them will understand, for example, the word mama.

There are quite a few words in Russian that are borrowed from English (List of English words of Russian origin *http://en.wikipedia.org/wiki/List_of_English_words_of_Russian _origin*) or from other European languages. Some of the words are pronounced almost the same as they are pronounced in English. Some words have some small differences in pronunciation, but you still will be able to recognize them.

Some words in Russian language have exactly the same pronunciation and meaning as English words. For instance, tennis – теннис, coffee – кофе, pizza – пицца, resume – резюме, passport – паспорт, visa – виза. Other words may sound the same in Russian as English words but have completely different meaning. For example, English word "look" in Russian language sounds exactly like "onion". Additionally, words may look very familiar and have the same meaning in both languages but they may not sound the same when you hear them with a stress on a different syllable.

The majority of geographical words (countries, cities, etc.) are pretty close to what they are in English: America – Америка, Las Vegas - Лас Вегас. As there are so many geographical words, you wouldn't find it here. Also, brand names and company names should never be translated: "The Beatles" will be always Beatles (Битлз) and "Red Hat" wouldn't be "Красная Шляпа" (Krasnaya Shlyapa) but "Ред Хэт". "Red Square" shouldn't be translated from Russian as "Red Square" but should be pronounsed as "Krasnaya ploshchad" "Красная площадь" (Russian researchers says that the name "Krasnaya" didn't come from color red but from the word "красивая" (handsome, lovely, or beautiful). Rock-n-Roll will be Рок-н-Ролл, Pop Music will be Поп-Музыка, and Ping Pong will still be Пинг-Понг.

Number of foreign words in everyday Russian speech from year to year increases exponentially. For example, лизинг (leasing), клинер (cleaner), маркет (market), офлайн (offline), пентхаус (penthouse), провайдер (provider), профайл (profile), резюме (resume), скриншот (screenshot), трафик (traffic), фандрайзинг (fundraising), франчайз (franchise), чизкейк (cheesecake), шоппинг (shopping), шоу (show), экстрим (extreme) and thousand more words.

The purpose of this book wasn't to write a research thesis about origin of everyday words, but to share the words that sound the same (or almost the same) in English and Russian languages and have similar meaning. Our language is changing at a terrifying rate. There are almost two thousand words here for you (wouldn't it be cool to tell your friends in a week that you know more than thousand Russian words?) It could be a good start to learn Russian language as you have already built a part of your Russian vocabulary.

Who This Book Is For

This book is for the reader who simply wants to have fun and expend their knowledge of a foreign language or for readers who wants to build Russian vocabulary based on similarity between English and Russian words quickly.

The Convention in This Book

Bold type shows the syllable we need to accentuate (stress) in order to pronounce the word correctly.

Why is Word/Letter Stress Important?

Word stress is not used in all languages. Japanese, for example, pronounce each syllable with equal emphasis. In English, word stress is part of the language. We just don't notice this rule. Let's take a word Internationaliza**t**ion. We know that the stress is on a last letter "a", not on any other vowel.

In Russian, the stress is a part of the language, too. Main rules about stress are the same in both languages:

- One word has only one stress.
- We can only stress vowels, not consonants.

When you learn a new word in any language, you need also learn its stress pattern. Otherwise nobody will understand what you are trying to say. For example, a Russian word ОРГАН. **О**РГАН is a body part and ОРГ**А**Н is a musical instrument. Some other examples: З**А**МОК (lock) – ЗАМ**О**К (castle), МУК**А** (flour) – М**У**КА (excruciation). Rules about stress in Russian language are rather complicated and there are many exceptions. But don't worry – it's always better to "feel" the language and everything else will come naturally.

THE RUSSIAN ALPHABET

The Russian alphabet (Russian: русский алфавит, transliteration: russkij alfavit) uses letters from the Cyrillic script and consists of 33 letters. You can listen to the Russian alphabet on the wikipedia website (http://en.wikipedia.org/wiki/Russian_alphabet).

А   Pronounced like the "a" in the word "drama" or "acrobat"

Б   Pronounced like the "b" in "boy"

В   Pronounced like the "v" in "vacuum"

Г   Pronounced like the "g" in "gadget"

Д   Pronounced like the "d" in "design"

Е   Pronounced like the "ye" in "yes".

Ё   Pronounced like "yo" in "yoghourt"

Ж   Pronounced like "s" in "leisure", "pleasure"

З   Pronounced like the "z" in "zebra"

И   Pronounced like the "i" in "index"

Й   Pronounced like the "y" in "yum"

К   Pronounced like the "c" in "calendar" or "k" in "kangaroo"

Л   Pronounced like the "l" in "love".

М   Pronounced like the "m" in mango.

Н   Pronounced like the "n" in "no"

О   When stressed, it is pronounced like the "o" in "shop". When un-stressed it is pronounced more like the letter "a".

П   Pronounced like the "p" in "park"

Р   Pronounced like the "r" in "radio"

С   Pronounced like the "s" in "secret"

Т   Pronounced like the "t" in "tiger"

У   Pronounced like the "oo" in "afternoon"

Ф   Pronounced like the "f" in "face"

Х   Pronounced like the "h" in "ham".

Ц   Pronounced like the "ts" sound in "tsunami"

Ч   Pronounced like the "ch" in "chair"

Ш   Pronounced like the "sh" in "shape"

Щ   You may find it difficult to hear the difference between "ш" and "щ". Try putting your tongue in the same position as you would to say "tia" in "dementia" but say "sh" instead.

Ъ   The 'Hard Sign' is rarely used. It indicates a slight pause between sylables.

Ы   Pronounced like the "i" in "bit" or "ill".

Ь   The 'Soft Sign' makes the previous letter 'soft'. Think of the "p" sound in the word "pew.

Э   Pronounced like the "e" in "eclair".

Ю   Pronounced like the "u" in "humor".

Я   Pronounced like the "ya" in "yahoo".

So let's begin!

A

ENGLISH	RUSSIAN	PRONONSIATION
ABORIGINAL	АБОРИГЕН	ABORIGEN
ACADEMY	АКАДЕМИЯ	AKADEMIYA
ACCENT	АКЦЕНТ	AKTSENT
ACCORD	АККОРД	AKKORD
ACCOUNT MANAGER	ЭККАУНТ-МЕНЕДЖЕР	AKKAUNT-MENEDZHER
ACOUSTICS	АКУСТИКА	AKUSTIKA
ACROBAT	АКРОБАТ	AKROBAT
ACT	АКТ	AKT
ACTIVE	АКТИВНЫЙ	AKTIVNYY
ACTOR	АКТЁР	AKTIOR
ACTRESS	АКТРИСА	AKTRISA
ADDRESS	АДРЕС	ADRES
ADMINISTRATION	АДМИНИСТРАЦИЯ	ADMINISTRATSIYA
ADMINISTRATOR	АДМИНИСТРАТОР	ADMINISTRATOR
ADMIRAL	АДМИРАЛ	ADMIRAL
ADVERTIZING	АДВЕРТАЙЗИНГ	ADVERTAYZING

ADVOCATE	АДВОКАТ	ADVOCAT
AEROBIC	АЭРОБИКА	AEROBIKA
AERODYNAMICS	АЭРОДИНАМИКА	AERODINAMIKA
AFFECT	АФФЕКТ	AFFEKT
AFTERSHOCK	АФТЕРШОК	AFTERSHOK
AGENT	АГЕНТ	AGENT
AGGRESSION	АГРЕССИЯ	AGRESSIYA
AIRPORT	АЭРОПОРТ	AEROPORT
ALBUM	АЛЬБОМ	AL'BOM
ALCOHOL	АЛКОГОЛЬ	ALKOGOL'
ALGEBRA	АЛГЕБРА	ALGEBRA
ALIBI	АЛИБИ	ALIBI
ALLERGY	АЛЛЕРГИЯ	ALLERGIYA
ALLEY	АЛЛЕЯ	ALLEYA
ALUMINIUM	АЛЮМИНИЙ	ALYUMINIY
AMBITION	АМБИЦИЯ	AMBITSIYA
ANACONDA	АНАКОНДА	ANAKONDA
ANAESTHESIA	АНЕСТЕЗИЯ	ANESTEZIYA
ANALOG	АНАЛОГ	ANALOG
ANALYSIS	АНАЛИЗ	ANALIZ
ANATOMY	АНАТОМИЯ	ANATOMIYA
ANCHOVY	АНЧОУС	ANCHOUS

Lawrence Burns

ANECDOTE	АНЕКДОТ	ANEKDOT
ANGEL	АНГЕЛ	ANGEL
ANONYM	АНОНИМ	ANONIM
ANTARCTICA	АНТАРКТИКА	ANTARKTIKA
ANTHOLOGY	АНТОЛОГИЯ	ANTOLOGIYA
ANTIBIOTIC	АНТИБИОТИК	ANTIBIOTIK
ANTICYCLONE	АНТИЦИКЛОН	ANTITSIKLON
APOCALYPSE	АПОКАЛИПСИС	APOKALIPSIS
APPETITE	АППЕТИТ	APPETIT
AQUARIUM	АКВАРИУМ	AKVARIUM
ARCHAEOLOGIST	АРХЕОЛОГ	ARKHEOLOG
ARCHITECT	АРХИТЕКТОР	ARKHITEKTOR
ARCHITECTURE	АРХИТЕКТУРА	ARKHITEKTURA
ARISTOCRAT	АРИСТОКРАТ	ARISTOKRAT
ARITHMETIC	АРИФМЕТИКА	ARIFMETIKA
ARMY	АРМИЯ	ARMIYA
AROMA	АРОМАТ	АРОМАT
ASBESTOS	АСБЕСТ	ASBEST
ASSISTANT	АССИСТЕНТ	ASSISTENT
ASSOCIATION	АССОЦИАЦИЯ	ASSOTSIATSIYA
ASTEROID	АСТЕРОИД	ASTEROID
ASTROLOGY	АСТРОЛОГИЯ	ASTROLOGIYA
ASYMMETRY	АСИММЕТРИЯ	ASIMMETRIYA

7

Kick-start Learning Russian:
2000 RUSSIAN Words You didn't Know You Knew

ATHEIST	АТЕИСТ	ATEIST
ATHLETE	АТЛЕТ	ATLET
ATMOSPHERE	АТМОСФЕРА	ATMOSFERA
AUCTION	АУКЦИОН	AUKTSION
AUDIO	АУДИО	AUDIO
AURA	АУРА	AURA
AUTHOR	АВТОР	AVTOR
AUTOBIOGRAPHY	АВТОБИОГРАФИЯ	AVTOBIOGRAFIYA
AUTOMATIC	АВТОМАТ	AVTOMAT
AUTOMOBILE	АВТОМОБИЛЬ	AVTOMOBIL'
AUTOPILOT	АВТОПИЛОТ	AVTOPILOT
AVIATION	АВИАЦИЯ	AVIATSIYA
AXIOM	АКСИОМА	AKSIOMA

B

ENGLISH	RUSSIAN	PRONONSIATION
BACKGROUND	БЭКГРАУНД	BEKGRAUND
BACTERIA	БАКТЕРИЯ	BAKTERIYA
BADMINTON	БАДМИНТОН	BADMINTON
BALANCE	БАЛАНС	BALANS
BALCONY	БАЛКОН	BALKON
BALLAD	БАЛЛАДА	BALLADA
BALLET	БАЛЕТ	BALET
BALM	БАЛЬЗАM	BAL'ZAM
BAMBOO	БАМБУК	BAMBUK
BANANA	БАНАН	BANAN
BANDIT	БАНДИТ	BANDIT
BANK	БАНК	BANK
BANKRUPT	БАНКРОТ	BANKROT
BAR	БАР	BAR
BARITONE	БАРИТОН	BARITON
BARMAN	БАРМЕН	BARMEN
BAROMETER	БАРОМЕТР	BAROMETR

BARRICADE	БАРРИКАДА	BARRIKADA
BASEBALL	БЕЙСБОЛ	BEYSBOL
BASKETBALL	БАСКЕТБОЛ	BASKETBOL
BASTION	БАСТИОН	BASTION
BATTERY	БАТАРЕЯ	BATAREYA
BENEFICIARY	БЕНЕФИЦИАР	BENEFITSIAR
BESTSELLER	БЕСТСЕЛЛЕР	BESTSELLER
BIATHLON	БИАТЛОН	BIATLON
BIKINI	БИКИНИ	BIKINI
BILLIARDS	БИЛЬЯРД	BIL'YARD
BILLION	БИЛЛИОН	BILLION
BINOCULARS	БИНОКЛЬ	BINOKL'
BIOGRAPHY	БИОГРАФИЯ	BIOGRAFIYA
BIOLOGY	БИОЛОГИЯ	BIOLOGIYA
BIOPSY	БИОПСИЯ	BIOPSIYA
BISCUIT	БИСКВИТ	BISKVIT
BLACKOUT	БЛЭКАУТ	BLEKAUT
BLOCK	БЛОК	BLOK
BLOCKADE	БЛОКАДА	BLOKADA
BLOCKBUSTER	БЛОКБАСТЕР	BLOKBASTER
BLOG	БЛОГ	BLOG
BLOGGER	БЛОГЕР	BLOGER

BLONDE	БЛОНДИН	BLONDIN
BLUES	БЛЮЗ	BLYUZ
BLUETOOTH	БЛЮТУС	BLYTYS
BOLSHEVIK	БОЛЬШЕВИК	BOL'SHEVIK
BOLT	БОЛТ	BOLT
BOMB	БОМБА	BOMBA
BONUS	БОНУС	BONUS
BOOMERANG	БУМЕРАНГ	BUMERANG
BOUDOIR	БУДУАР	BUDUAR
BOURGEOISIE	БУРЖУАЗИЯ	BURZHUAZIYA
BOUTIQUE	БУТИК	BUTIK
BOXING	БОКС	BOKS
BOYCOTT	БОЙКОТ	BOYKOT
BOYFRIEND	БОЙФРЕНД	BOYFREND
BREEZE	БРИЗ	BRIZ
BRIEFING	БРИФИНГ	BRIFING
BRONCHITIS	БРОНХИТ	BRONKHIT
BROTHER	БРАТ	BRAT
BUDDHISM	БУДДИЗМ	BUDDIZM
BUFFET	БУФЕТ	BUFET
BULLDOG	БУЛЬДОГ	BUL'DOG
BUMPER	БАМПЕР	BAMPER
BUNGALOW	БУНГАЛО	BUNGALO

Kick-start Learning Russian:
2000 RUSSIAN Words You didn't Know You Knew

BUSINESS	БИЗНЕС	BIZNES
BUSINESSMAN	БИЗНЕСМЕН	BIZNESMEN
BUY BACK	БАЙБЭК	BAYBEK

C

ENGLISH	RUSSIAN	PRONONSIATION
CABARET	КАБАРЕ	KABARE
CABIN	КАБИНА	KABINA
CABRIOLET	КАБРИОЛЕТ	KABRIOLET
CACTUS	КАКТУС	KAKTUS
CAFE	КАФЕ	KAFE
CAFFEINE	КОФЕИН	KOFEIN
CAKE	КЕКС	KEKS
CALAMARY	КАЛЬМАР	KAL'MAR
CALCULATOR	КАЛЬКУЛЯТОР	KAL'KULYATOR
CALENDAR	КАЛЕНДАРЬ	KALENDAR'
CALENDULA	КАЛЕНДУЛА	KALENDULA
CALIBRE	КАЛИБР	KALIBR
CALLIGRAPHY	КАЛЛИГРАФИЯ	KALLIGRAFIYA
CALORIE	КАЛОРИЯ	KALORIYA
CAMELLIA	КАМЕЛИЯ	KAMELIYA
CAMOUFLAGE	КАМУФЛЯЖ	KAMUFLYAZH
CAMPAIGN	КАМПАНИЯ	KAMPANIYA

13

CAMPING	КЕМПИНГ	KEMPING
CANDIDATE	КАНДИДАТ	KANDIDAT
CANISTER	КАНИСТРА	KANISTRA
CANNIBAL	КАННИБАЛ	KANNIBAL
CANOE	КАНОЭ	KANOE
CANOEIST	КАНОИСТ	KANOIST
CAPITALISM	КАПИТАЛИЗМ	KAPITALIZM
CAPITULATION	КАПИТУЛЯЦИЯ	KAPITULYATSIYA
CAPSULE	КАПСУЛА	KAPSULA
CAPTAIN	КАПИТАН	KAPITAN
CARAT	КАРАТ	KARAT
CARBINE	КАРАБИН	KARABIN
CARBUNCLE	КАРБУНКУЛ	KARBUNKUL
CARBURETOR	КАРБЮРАТОР	KARBYURATOR
CARCINOGEN	КАНЦЕРОГЕН	KANTSEROGEN
CARDINAL	КАРДИНАЛ	KARDINAL
CARDIO	КАРДИО	KARDIO
CARDIOGRAM	КАРДИОГРАММА	KARDIOGRAMMA
CARDIOLOGIST	КАРДИОЛОГ	KARDIOLOG
CAREER	КАРЬЕРА	KAR'YERA
CARICATURE	КАРИКАТУРА	KARIKATURA
CARICATURIST	КАРИКАТУРИСТ	KARIKATURIST

CARMINE	КАРМИН	KARMIN
CAROTENE	КАРОТИН	KAROTIN
CASCADE	КАСКАД	KASKAD
CASE	КЕЙС	KEYS
CASINO	КАЗИНО	KAZINO
CATALOGUE	КАТАЛОГ	KATALOG
CATALYST	КАТАЛИЗАТОР	KATALIZATOR
CATAPULT	КАТАПУЛЬТА	KATAPUL'TA
CATASTROPHE	КАТАСТРОФА	KATASTROFA
CATEGORY	КАТЕГОРИЯ	KATEGORIYA
CATHETER	КАТЕТЕР	KATETER
CATHOLICS	КАТОЛИК	KATOLIK
CELLOPHANE	ЦЕЛЛОФАН	TSELLOFAN
CELLULOID	ЦЕЛЛУЛОИД	TSELLULOID
CELLULOSE	ЦЕЛЛЮЛОЗА	TSELLYULOZA
CEMENT	ЦЕМЕНТ	TSEMENT
CENTER	ЦЕНТР	TSENTR
CENTIMETER	САНТИМЕТР	SANTIMETR
CERAMICS	КЕРАМИКА	KERAMIKA
CEREMONY	ЦЕРЕМОНИЯ	TSEREMONIYA
CERTIFICATE	СЕРТИФИКАТ	SERTIFIKAT
CHAMELEON	ХАМЕЛЕОН	KHAMELEON
CHAMPAGNE	ШАМПАНСКОЕ	SHAMPANSKOYE

CHAMPIGNON	ШАМПИНЬОН	SHAMPIN'ON
CHAMPION	ЧЕМПИОН	CHEMPION
CHANCE	ШАНС	SHANS
CHANSON	ШАНСОНЬЕ	SHANSON'YE
CHAOS	ХАОС	KHAOS
CHARACTER	ХАРАКТЕР	KHARAKTER
CHASSIS	ШАССИ	SHASSI
CHEESECAKE	ЧИЗКЕЙК	CHIZKEYK
CHEF	ШЕФ	SHEF
CHEQUE	ЧЕК	CHEK
CHIGNON	ШИНЬОН	SHIN'ON
CHILL OUT	ЧИЛАУТ	CHILAUT
CHINCHILLA	ШИНШИЛЛА	SHINSHILLA
CHLOROPHYLL	ХЛОРОФИЛЛ	KHLOROFILL
CHOCOLATE	ШОКОЛАД	SHOKOLAD
CHOREOGRAPHER	ХОРЕОГРАФ	KHOREOGRAF
CHOREOGRAPHY	ХОРЕОГРАФИЯ	KHOREOGRAFIYA
CHRONICLE	ХРОНИКА	KHRONIKA
CHRONOLOGY	ХРОНОЛОГИЯ	KHRONOLOGIYA
CHRONOMETER	ХРОНОМЕТР	KHRONOMETR
CHRYSANTHEMUM	ХРИЗАНТЕМА	KHRIZANTEMA
CIGARETTE	СИГАРЕТА	SIGARETA

CINEMATOGRAPH	КИНЕМАТОГРАФ	KINEMATOGRAF
CIRCUS	ЦИРК	TSIRK
CISTERN	ЦИСТЕРНА	TSISTERNA
CITATION	ЦИТАТА	TSITATA
CITRUS	ЦИТРУС	TSITRUS
CIVILIZATION	ЦИВИЛИЗАЦИЯ	TSIVILIZATSIYA
CLAN	КЛАН	KLAN
CLASS	КЛАСС	KLASS
CLASSICS	КЛАССИКА	KLASSIKA
CLEANER	КЛИНЕР	KLINER
CLEANING	КЛИНИНГ	KLINING
CLICHE	КЛИШЕ	KLISHE
CLIENT	КЛИЕНТ	KLIYENT
CLIMATE	КЛИМАТ	KLIMAT
CLIPS	КЛИПСЫ	KLIPSY
CLOWN	КЛОУН	KLOUN
CLUB	КЛУБ	KLUB
COALITION	КОАЛИЦИЯ	KOALITSIYA
COBRA	КОБРА	KOBRA
COCAINE	КОКАИН	KOKAIN
COCKTAIL	КОКТЕЙЛЬ	KOKTEYL'
COCOA	КАКАО	KAKAO
CODE	КОД	KOD

Kick-start Learning Russian:
2000 RUSSIAN Words You didn't Know You Knew

COEFFICIENT	КОЭФФИЦИЕНТ	KOEFFITSIYENT
COFFEE	КОФЕ	KOFE
COFFEE BREAK	КОФЕ-БРЕЙК	KOFE-BREYK
COGNAC	КОНЬЯК	KON'YAK
COLIBRI	КОЛИБРИ	KOLIBRI
COLLAGE	КОЛЛАЖ	KOLLAZH
COLLEAGUE	КОЛЛЕГА	KOLLEGA
COLLECTION	КОЛЛЕКЦИЯ	KOLLEKTSIYA
COLLECTOR	КОЛЛЕКТОР	KOLLEKTOR
COLLEGE	КОЛЛЕДЖ	KOLLEDZH
COLLOID	КОЛЛОИД	KOLLOID
COLLOQUIUM	КОЛЛОКВИУМ	KOLLOKVIUM
COLOUR	КОЛЕР	KOLER
COLT	КОЛЬТ	KOL'T
COLUMN	КОЛОННА	KOLONNA
COMEDY	КОМЕДИЯ	KOMEDIYA
COMET	КОМЕТА	KOMETA
COMFORT	КОМФОРТ	KOMFORT
COMICS	КОМИКС	KOMIKS
COMMANDANT	КОМЕНДАНТ	KOMENDANT
COMMANDER	КОМАНДИР	KOMANDIR
COMMENT	КОММЕНТ	KOMMENT

COMMENTATOR	КОММЕНТАТОР	KOMMENTATOR
COMMERCE	КОММЕРЦИЯ	KOMMERTSIYA
COMMISSION	КОМИССИЯ	KOMISSIYA
COMMITTEE	КОМИТЕТ	KOMITET
COMMUNISM	КОММУНИЗМ	KOMMUNIZM
COMPACT DISC	КОМПАКТ-ДИСК	KOMPAKT-DISK
COMPANION	КОМПАНЬОН	KOMPAN'ON
COMPANY	КОМПАНИЯ	KOMPANIYA
COMPASS	КОМПАС	KOMPAS
COMPENSATION	КОМПЕНСАЦИЯ	KOMPENSATSIYA
COMPETENCE	КОМПЕТЕНЦИЯ	KOMPETENTSIYA
COMPLEX	КОМПЛЕКС	KOMPLEKS
COMPLIMENT	КОМПЛИМЕНТ	KOMPLIMENT
COMPONENT	КОМПОНЕНТ	KOMPONENT
COMPOSER	КОМПОЗИТОР	KOMPOZITOR
COMPOST	КОМПОСТ	KOMPOST
COMPRESS	КОМПРЕСС	KOMPRESS
COMPRESSOR	КОМПРЕССОР	KOMPRESSOR
COMPROMISE	КОМПРОМИСС	KOMPROMISS
COMPUTER	КОМПЬЮТЕР	KOMP'YUTER
CONCENTRATE	КОНЦЕНТРАТ	KONTSENTRAT
CONCENTRATION	КОНЦЕНТРАЦИЯ	KONTSENTRATSIYA
CONCEPT	КОНЦЕПЦИЯ	KONTSEPTSIYA

Kick-start Learning Russian:
2000 RUSSIAN Words You didn't Know You Knew

CONCERN	КОНЦЕРН	KONTSERN
CONCERT	КОНЦЕРТ	KONTSERT
CONCESSION	КОНЦЕССИЯ	KONTSESSIYA
CONCIERGE	КОНСЬЕРЖ	KONS'YERZH
CONDENSATE	КОНДЕНСАТ	KONDENSAT
CONDENSER	КОНДЕНСАТОР	KONDENSATOR
CONDITIONER	КОНДИЦИОНЕР	KONDITSIONER
CONDUCTOR	КОНДУКТОР	KONDUKTOR
CONE	КОНУС	KONUS
CONFEDERATION	КОНФЕДЕРАЦИЯ	KONFEDERATSIYA
CONFERENCE	КОНФЕРЕНЦИЯ	KONFERENTSIYA
CONFETTI	КОНФЕТТИ	KONFETTI
CONFLICT	КОНФЛИКТ	KONFLIKT
CONGLOMERATE	КОНГЛОМЕРАТ	KONGLOMERAT
CONGRESS	КОНГРЕСС	KONGRESS
CONGRESSMAN	КОНГРЕССМЕН	KONGRESSMEN
CONJUNCTIVITIS	КОНЪЮНКТИВИТ	KON"YUNKTIVIT
CONSERVATORY	КОНСЕРВАТОРИЯ	KONSERVATORIYA
CONSILIUM	КОНСИЛИУМ	KONSILIUM
CONSISTENCY	КОНСИСТЕНЦИЯ	KONSISTENTSIYA
CONSOLE	КОНСОЛЬ	KONSOL'
CONSPIRACY	КОНСПИРАЦИЯ	KONSPIRATSIYA

CONSPIRATOR	КОНСПИРАТОР	KONSPIRATOR
CONSTITUTION	КОНСТИТУЦИЯ	KONSTITUTSIYA
CONSTRUCTION	КОНСТРУКЦИЯ	KONSTRUKTSIYA
CONSUL	КОНСУЛ	KONSUL
CONSULATE	КОНСУЛЬСТВО	KONSUL'STVO
CONSULTANT	КОНСУЛЬТАНТ	KONSUL'TANT
CONSULTATION	КОНСУЛЬТАЦИЯ	KONSUL'TATSIA
CONTACT	КОНТАКТ	KONTAKT
CONTACT CENTER	КОНТАКТ-ЦЕНТР	KONTAKT-TSENTR
CONTAINER	КОНТЕЙНЕР	KONTEYNER
CONTENT	КОНТЕНТ	KONTENT
CONTEXT	КОНТЕКСТ	KONTEKST
CONTINENT	КОНТИНЕНТ	KONTINENT
CONTINGENT	КОНТИНГЕНТ	KONTINGENT
CONTOUR	КОНТУР	KONTUR
CONTRACEPTIVE	КОНТРАЦЕПТИВ	KONTRATSEPTIV
CONTRACT	КОНТРАКТ	KONTRAKT
CONTRIBUTION	КОНТРИБУЦИЯ	KONTRIBUTSIYA
CONTROL	КОНТРОЛЬ	KONTROL'
CONVENTION	КОНВЕНЦИЯ	KONVENTSIYA
CONVERSION	КОНВЕРСИЯ	KONVERSIYA
CONVOY	КОНВОЙ	KONVOY
COOPERATIVE	КООПЕРАТИВ	KOOPERATIV

COORDINATE	КООРДИНАТА	KOORDINATA
COORDINATOR	КООРДИНАТОР	KOORDINATOR
COPYRIGHT	КОПИРАЙТ	KOPIRAYT
CORONATION	КОРОНАЦИЯ	KORONATSIYA
CORPORATION	КОРПОРАЦИЯ	KORPORATSIYA
CORRECTOR	КОРРЕКТОР	KORREKTOR
CORRESPONDENCE	КОРРЕСПОНДЕНЦИЯ	KORRESPONDENTSIYA
CORRESPONDENT	КОРРЕСПОНДЕНТ	KORRESPONDENT
CORROSION	КОРРОЗИЯ	KORROZIYA
CORRUPTION	КОРРУПЦИЯ	KORRUPTSIYA
CORSAGE	КОРСАЖ	KORSAZH
CORSET	КОРСЕТ	KORSET
CORUND	КОРУНД	KORUND
CORVETTE	КОРВЕТ	KORVET
COSMETICS	КОСМЕТИКА	KOSMETIKA
COSMETOLOGIST	КОСМЕТОЛОГ	KOSMETOLOG
COSTUME	КОСТЮМ	KOSTYUM
COTTAGE	КОТТЕДЖ	KOTTEDZH
COURIER	КУРЬЕР	KURЬER
COURSE	КУРС	KURS
COURT	КОРТ	KORT
COUSIN	КУЗЕН	KUZEN

COUTURE	КУТЮРЬЕ	KUTYUR'Y**E**
COWBOY	КОВБОЙ	KOVB**O**Y
CRAB	КРАБ	KR**A**B
CRACKING	КРЕКИНГ	KR**E**KING
CRATER	КРАТЕР	KR**A**TER
CREAM	КРЕМ	KR**E**M
CREDIT	КРЕДИТ	KRED**I**T
CREMATION	КРЕМАЦИЯ	KREM**A**TSIYA
CREMATORIUM	КРЕМАТОРИЙ	KREMAT**O**RIY
CRIMINALISTICS	КРИМИНАЛИСТИКА	KRIMINAL**I**STIKA
CRISIS	КРИЗИС	KR**I**ZIS
CRITIC	КРИТИК	KR**I**TIK
CRITIQUE	КРИТИКА	KR**I**TIKA
CROCODILE	КРОКОДИЛ	KROKOD**I**L
CROCUS	КРОКУС	KR**O**KUS
CROQUET	КРОКЕТ	KROK**E**T
CROSSWORD	КРОССВОРД	KROSSV**O**RD
CRYPTOGRAPHY	КРИПТОГРАФИЯ	KRIPTOGR**A**FIYA
CRYSTAL	КРИСТАЛЛ	KRIST**A**LL
CRYSTALLOGRAPHY	КРИСТАЛЛОГРАФИЯ	KRISTALLOGR**A**FIYA
CYBERNETICS	КИБЕРНЕТИКА	KIBERN**E**TIKA
CYCLE	ЦИКЛ	TS**I**KL
CYCLONE	ЦИКЛОН	TSIKL**O**N

CYLINDER	ЦИЛИНДР	TSILINDR
CYPRESS	КИПАРИС	KIPARIS
CYRILLIC	КИРИЛЛИЦА	KIRILLITSA

D

ENGLISH	RUSSIAN	PRONONSIATION
DATE	ДАТА	DATA
DAY	ДЕНЬ	DEN'
DE FACTO	ДЕ-ФАКТО	DE-FAKTO
DEACTIVATION	ДЕЗАКТИВАЦИЯ	DEZAKTIVATSIYA
DEAD-LINE	ДЕДЛАЙН	DEDLAYN
DEALER	ДИЛЕР	DILER
DEBUT	ДЕБЮТ	DEBYUT
DECIBEL (DB)	ДЕЦИБЕЛ	DETSIBEL
DECIMETER	ДЕЦИМЕТР	DETSIMETR
DECLARATION	ДЕКЛАРАЦИЯ	DEKLARATSIYA
DECORATIONS	ДЕКОРАЦИЯ	DEKORATSIYA
DECORATOR	ДЕКОРАТОР	DEKORATOR
DEDUCTION	ДЕДУКЦИЯ	DEDUKTSIYA
DEFECT	ДЕФЕКТ	DEFEKT
DEFECTIVE	ДЕФЕКТНЫЙ	DEFEKTNYY
DEFICIT	ДЕФИЦИТ	DEFITSIT
DEGENERATION	ДЕГЕНЕРАЦИЯ	DEGENERATSIYA

DELEGATE	ДЕЛЕГАТ	DELEGAT
DEMAGOGUE	ДЕМАГОГ	DEMAGOG
DEMOCRACY	ДЕМОКРАТИЯ	DEMOKRATIYA
DEMOCRAT	ДЕМОКРАТ	DEMOKRAT
DEMOGRAPHICS	ДЕМОГРАФИЯ	DEMOGRAFIYA
DEMON	ДЕМОН	DEMON
DEMONSTRATION	ДЕМОНСТРАЦИЯ	DEMONSTRATSIYA
DEMONSTRATOR	ДЕМОНСТРАТОР	DEMONSTRATOR
DENTIST	ДАНТИСТ	DANTIST
DEODORANT	ДЕЗОДОРАНТ	DEZODORANT
DEPARTMENT	ДЕПАРТАМЕНТ	DEPARTAMENT
DEPORTATION	ДЕПОРТАЦИЯ	DEPORTATSIYA
DEPOSIT	ДЕПОЗИТ	DEPOZIT
DEPOT	ДЕПО	DEPO
DEPRESSION	ДЕПРЕССИЯ	DEPRESSIYA
DERMATOLOGIST	ДЕРМАТОЛОГ	DERMATOLOG
DERMATOLOGY	ДЕРМАТОЛОГИЯ	DERMATOLOGIYA
DESIGN	ДИЗАЙН	DIZAYN
DESIGNER	ДИЗАЙНЕР	DIZAYNER
DESSERT	ДЕСЕРТ	DESERT
DETECTIVE	ДЕТЕКТИВ	DETEKTIV
DETECTOR	ДЕТЕКТОР	DETEKTOR

DETONATION	ДЕТОНАЦИЯ	DETONATSIYA
DETONATOR	ДЕТОНАТОР	DETONATOR
DEVELOPER	ДЕВЕЛОПЕР	DEVELOPER
DEVELOPMENT	ДЕВЕЛОПМЕНТ	DEVELOPMENT
DEVICE	ДЕВАЙС	DEVAYS
DIABETES	ДИАБЕТ	DIABET
DIABETIC	ДИАБЕТИК	DIABETIK
DIADEM	ДИАДЕМА	DIADEMA
DIAGNOSIS	ДИАГНОЗ	DIAGNOZ
DIAGNOSTICS	ДИАГНОСТИКА	DIAGNOSTIKA
DIAGONAL	ДИАГОНАЛЬ	DIAGONAL'
DIAGRAM	ДИАГРАММА	DIAGRAMMA
DIALECT	ДИАЛЕКТ	DIALEKT
DIALOGUE	ДИАЛОГ	DIALOG
DIAMETER	ДИАМЕТР	DIAMETR
DIAPHRAGM	ДИАФРАГМА	DIAFRAGMA
DICTATION	ДИКТАНТ	DIKTANT
DICTATOR	ДИКТАТОР	DIKTATOR
DICTION	ДИКЦИЯ	DIKTSIYA
DICTOPHONE	ДИКТОФОН	DIKTOFON
DIELECTRIC	ДИЭЛЕКТРИК	DIELEKTRIK
DIESEL	ДИЗЕЛЬ	DIZEL'
DIET	ДИЕТА	DIYETA

DIFFERENTIAL	ДИФФЕРЕНЦИАЛ	DIFFERENTSIAL
DIFFRACTION	ДИФРАКЦИЯ	DIFRAKTSIYA
DIFFUSION	ДИФФУЗИЯ	DIFFUZIYA
DILEMMA	ДИЛЕММА	DILEMMA
DINGO	ДИНГО	DINGO
DINOSAUR	ДИНОЗАВР	DINOZAVR
DIODE	ДИОД	DIOD
DIORAMA	ДИОРАМА	DIORAMA
DIOXIDE	ДИОКСИД	DIOKSID
DIPLOMA	ДИПЛОМ	DIPLOM
DIPLOMAT	ДИПЛОМАТ	DIPLOMAT
DIRECTOR	ДИРЕКТОР	DIREKTOR
DIRECTORY	ДИРЕКТОРИЯ	DIREKTORIYA
DISC	ДИСК	DISK
DISC JOCKEY	ДИСК-ЖОКЕЙ	DISK-ZHOKEY
DISCIPLINE	ДИСЦИПЛИНА	DISTSIPLINA
DISCO	ДИСКО	DISKO
DISCOMFORT	ДИСКОМФОРТ	DISKOMFORT
DISCOUNT	ДИСКАУНТ	DISKAUNT
DISCRIMINATION	ДИСКРИМИНАЦИЯ	DISKRIMINATSIYA
DISCUSSION	ДИСКУССИЯ	DISKUSSIYA
DISINFECTION	ДЕЗИНФЕКЦИЯ	DEZINFEKTSIYA

Lawrence Burns

DISKETTE	ДИСКЕТА	DISKETA
DISPLAY	ДИСПЛЕЙ	DISPLEY
DISSIMILATION	ДИССИМИЛЯЦИЯ	DISSIMILYATSIYA
DISTANCE	ДИСТАНЦИЯ	DISTANTSIYA
DISTILLATION	ДИСТИЛЛЯЦИЯ	DISTILLYATSIYA
DIVIDEND	ДИВИДЕНД	DIVIDEND
DIVING	ДАЙВИНГ	DAYVING
DOCK	ДОК	DOK
DOCTOR	ДОКТОР	DOKTOR
DOCTRINE	ДОКТРИНА	DOKTRINA
DOCUMENT	ДОКУМЕНТ	DOKUMENT
DOGMA	ДОГМА	DOGMA
DOLPHIN	ДЕЛЬФИН	DEL'FIN
DOMINANT	ДОМИНАНТА	DOMINANTA
DOMINO	ДОМИНО	DOMINO
DOSE	ДОЗА	DOZA
DOSSIER	ДОСЬЕ	DOS'YE
DOUBLE	ДУБЛЬ	DUBL'
DOWNSHIFTING	ДАУНШИФТИНГ	DAUNSHIFTING
DRAFT	ДРАФТ	DRAFT
DRAGON	ДРАКОН	DRAKON
DRAMA	ДРАМА	DRAMA
DRESS CODE	ДРЕСС-КОД	DRESS-KOD

29

DRIFT	ДРЕЙФ	DREYF
DRILL	ДРЕЛЬ	DREL'
DRIVE	ДРАЙВ	DRAYV
DRIVER	ДРАЙВЕР	DRAYVER
DUET	ДУЭТ	DUET
DYNAMICS	ДИНАМИКА	DINAMIKA
DYNAMITE	ДИНАМИТ	DINAMIT
DYNAMO	ДИНАМО	DINAMO
DYNASTY	ДИНАСТИЯ	DINASTIYA
DYSTROPHY	ДИСТРОФИЯ	DISTROFIYA

E

ENGLISH	RUSSIAN	PRONONSIATION
ECCENTRIC	ЭКСЦЕНТРИК	EKSTSENTRIK
ECLAIR	ЭКЛЕР	EKLER
ECONOMICS	ЭКОНОМИКА	EKONOMIKA
EDELWEISS	ЭДЕЛЬВЕЙС	EDEL'VEYS
EFFECT	ЭФФЕКТ	EFFEKT
EGOCENTRISM	ЭГОЦЕНТРИЗМ	EGOTSENTRIZM
EGOISM	ЭГОИЗМ	EGOIZM
EGOIST	ЭГОИСТ	EGOIST
ELECTRICITY	ЭЛЕКТРИЧЕСТВО	ELEKTRICHESTVO
ELECTRODE	ЭЛЕКТРОД	ELEKTROD
ELECTRODYNAMICS	ЭЛЕКТРОДИНАМИКА	ELEKTRODINAMIKA
ELECTROLYSIS	ЭЛЕКТРОЛИЗ	ELEKTROLIZ
ELECTROMAGNET	ЭЛЕКТРОМАГНИТ	ELEKTROMAGNIT
ELECTROMAGNETISM	ЭЛЕКТРОМАГНЕТИЗМ	ELEKTROMAGNETIZM
ELECTROMOTOR	ЭЛЕКТРОМОТОР	ELEKTROMOTOR
ELECTRON	ЭЛЕКТРОН	ELEKTRON
ELECTRONICS	ЭЛЕКТРОНИКА	ELEKTRONIKA

31

Kick-start Learning Russian:
2000 RUSSIAN Words You didn't Know You Knew

ELECTROSHOCK	ЭЛЕКТРОШОК	ELEKTROSHOK
ELECTROTHERAPY	ЭЛЕКТРОТЕРАПИЯ	ELEKTROTERAPIYA
ELEGY	ЭЛЕГИЯ	ELEGIYA
ELEMENT	ЭЛЕМЕНТ	ELEMENT
ELEVATOR	ЭЛЕВАТОР	ELEVATOR
ELITE	ЭЛИТА	ELITA
ELIXIR	ЭЛИКСИР	ELIKSIR
ELLIPSE	ЭЛЛИПС	ELLIPS
EMANCIPATION	ЭМАНСИПАЦИЯ	EMANSIPATSIYA
EMBARGO	ЭМБАРГО	EMBARGO
EMBLEM	ЭМБЛЕМА	EMBLEMA
EMBRYO	ЭМБРИОН	EMBRION
EMBRYOLOGY	ЭМБРИОЛОГИЯ	EMBRIOLOGIYA
EMIGRATION	ЭМИГРАЦИЯ	EMIGRATSIYA
EMISSION	ЭМИССИЯ	EMISSIYA
EMOTION	ЭМОЦИЯ	EMOTSIYA
EMPIRICISM	ЭМПИРИЗМ	EMPIRIZM
EMULSION	ЭМУЛЬСИЯ	EMUL'SIYA
ENAMEL	ЭМАЛЬ	EMAL'
ENCYCLOPEDIA	ЭНЦИКЛОПЕДИЯ	ENTSIKLOPEDIYA
ENDOCRINOLOGY	ЭНДОКРИНОЛОГИЯ	ENDOKRINOLOGIYA
ENDOSCOPE	ЭНДОСКОП	ENDOSKOP

ENERGY	ЭНЕРГИЯ	ENERGIYA
ENGINEER	ИНЖЕНЕР	INZHENER
ENTHUSIASM	ЭНТУЗИАЗМ	ENTUZIAZM
ENTHUSIAST	ЭНТУЗИАСТ	ENTUZIAST
ENTOMOLOGY	ЭНТОМОЛОГИЯ	ENTOMOLOGIYA
EPICENTER	ЭПИЦЕНТР	EPITSENTR
EPIDEMIC	ЭПИДЕМИЯ	EPIDEMIYA
EPIDEMIOLOGY	ЭПИДЕМИОЛОГИЯ	EPIDEMIOLOGIYA
EPIGRAM	ЭПИГРАММА	EPIGRAMMA
EPIGRAPH	ЭПИГРАФ	EPIGRAF
EPILEPSY	ЭПИЛЕПСИЯ	EPILEPSIYA
EPILOGUE	ЭПИЛОГ	EPILOG
EPISODE	ЭПИЗОД	EPIZOD
EPITAPH	ЭПИТАФИЯ	EPITAFIYA
EPITHET	ЭПИТЕТ	EPITET
EPOCH	ЭПОХА	EPOKHA
EPOS	ЭПОС	EPOS
EQUATOR	ЭКВАТОР	EKVATOR
EQUIVALENT	ЭКВИВАЛЕНТ	EKVIVALENT
ERA	ЭРА	ERA
EROSION	ЭРОЗИЯ	EROZIYA
EROTIC	ЭРОТИКА	EROTIKA
ERUDIT	ЭРУДИТ	ERUDIT

ERYTHROCYTES	ЭРИТРОЦИТЫ	ERITROTSITY
ESCALATOR	ЭСКАЛАТОР	ESKALATOR
ESCORT	ЭСКОРТ	ESKORT
ESKIMO	ЭСКИМО	ESKIMO
ESPERANTO	ЭСПЕРАНТО	ESPERANTO
ESSAY	ЭССЕ	ESSE
ESSENCE	ЭССЕНЦИЯ	ESSENTSIYA
ESTHETICS	ЭСТЕТИКА	ESTETIKA
ESTIMATE	ЭСТИМЕЙТ	ESTIMEYT
ETHICS	ЭТИКА	ETIKA
ETHNOGRAPHY	ЭТНОГРАФИЯ	ETNOGRAFIYA
ETHOLOGY	ЭТОЛОГИЯ	ETOLOGIYA
ETYMOLOGY	ЭТИМОЛОГИЯ	ETIMOLOGIYA
EUCALYPTUS	ЭВКАЛИПТ	EVKALIPT
EUROPE	ЕВРОПА	YEVROPA
EVACUATION	ЭВАКУАЦИЯ	EVAKUATSIYA
EVOLUTION	ЭВОЛЮЦИЯ	EVOLYUTSIYA
EXCAVATOR	ЭКСКАВАТОР	EKSKAVATOR
EXCESS	ЭКСЦЕСС	EKSTSESS
EXCURSION	ЭКСКУРСИЯ	EKSKURSIYA
EXECUTION	ЭКЗЕКУЦИЯ	EKZEKUTSIYA
EXHUMATION	ЭКСГУМАЦИЯ	EKSGUMATSIYA

EXOTICS	ЭКЗОТИКА	EKZOTIKA
EXPATRIATE	ЭКСПАТ	EKSPAT
EXPEDITION	ЭКСПЕДИЦИЯ	EKSPEDITSIYA
EXPERIMENT	ЭКСПЕРИМЕНТ	EKSPERIMENT
EXPERIMENTALIST	ЭКСПЕРИМЕНТАТОР	EKSPERIMENTATOR
EXPERT	ЭКСПЕРТ	EKSPERT
EXPERTISE	ЭКСПЕРТИЗА	EKSPERTIZA
EXPLOITATION	ЭКСПЛУАТАЦИЯ	EKSPLUATATSIYA
EXPONENT	ЭКСПОНЕНТА	EKSPONENTA
EXPORT	ЭКСПОРТ	EKSPORT
EXPRESS	ЭКСПРЕСС	EKSPRESS
EXTRACT	ЭКСТРАКТ	EKSTRAKT
EXTREME	ЭКСТРИМ	EKSTRIM
EXTREMISM	ЭКСТРЕМИЗМ	EKSTREMIZM
EXTREMIST	ЭКСТРЕМИСТ	EKSTREMIST

F

ENGLISH	RUSSIAN	PRONONSIATION
FACADE	ФАСАД	FASAD
FACT	ФАКТ	FAKT
FACTOR	ФАКТОР	FAKTOR
FACULTY	ФАКУЛЬТЕТ	FAKUL'TET
FAKE	ФЕЙК	FEYK
FALSE START	ФАЛЬСТАРТ	FAL'START
FALSIFICATION	ФАЛЬСИФИКАЦИЯ	FAL'SIFIKATSIYA
FANATICISM	ФАНАТИЗМ	FANATIZM
FANFARE	ФАНФАРА	FANFARA
FANTASY	ФАНТАЗИЯ	FANTAZIYA
FARM	ФЕРМА	FERMA
FARMER	ФЕРМЕР	FERMER
FASCISM	ФАШИЗМ	FASHIZM
FASCIST	ФАШИСТ	FASHIST
FAST FOOD	ФАСТ-ФУД	FAST-FUD
FATALISM	ФАТАЛИЗМ	FATALIZM
FATALIST	ФАТАЛИСТ	FATALIST

FAVORITE	ФАВОРИТ	FAVORIT
FAX	ФАКС	FAKS
FEDERATION	ФЕДЕРАЦИЯ	FEDERATSIYA
FEEDBACK	ФИДБЭК	FIDBEK
FEMINISM	ФЕМИНИЗМ	FEMINIZM
FEMINIST	ФЕМИНИСТ	FEMINIST
FESTIVAL	ФЕСТИВАЛЬ	FESTIVAL'
FICTION	ФИКЦИЯ	FIKTSIYA
FIGURE	ФИГУРА	FIGURA
FILE	ФАЙЛ	FAYL
FILIBUSTER	ФЛИБУСТЬЕР	FLIBUST'YER
FILLET	ФИЛЕ	FILE
FILM	ФИЛЬМ	FIL'M
FILTER	ФИЛЬТР	FIL'TR
FILTRATION	ФИЛЬТРАЦИЯ	FIL'TRATSIYA
FINALE	ФИНАЛ	FINAL
FINALIST	ФИНАЛИСТ	FINALIST
FINANCE	ФИНАНСЫ	FINANSY
FINISH	ФИНИШ	FINISH
FIRM	ФИРМА	FIRMA
FLACON	ФЛАКОН	FLAKON
FLAG	ФЛАГ	FLAG

FOLKLORE	ФОЛЬКЛОР	FOL'KLOR
FOOD COURT	ФУД-КОРТ	FUD-KORT
FOOTBALL	ФУТБОЛ	FUTBOL
FORM	ФОРМА	FORMA
FORMALISM	ФОРМАЛИЗМ	FORMALIZM
FORMALIST	ФОРМАЛИСТ	FORMALIST
FORMAT	ФОРМАТ	FORMAT
FORMULA	ФОРМУЛА	FORMULA
FORT	ФОРТ	FORT
FORTUNA	ФОРТУНА	FORTUNA
FORUM	ФОРУМ	FORUM
FOUNDATION	ФУНДАМЕНТ	FUNDAMENT
FOUNTAIN	ФОНТАН	FONTAN
FOX TERRIER	ФОКСТЕРЬЕР	FOKSTER'YER
FOXTROT	ФОКСТРОТ	FOKSTROT
FOYER	ФОЙЕ	FOYYE
FRACTION	ФРАКЦИЯ	FRAKTSIYA
FRAGMENT	ФРАГМЕНТ	FRAGMENT
FRANCHISE	ФРАНЧАЙЗ	FRANCHAYZ
FREAK	ФРИК	FRIK
FREELANCER	ФРИЛАНСЕР	FRILANSER
FRIGATE	ФРЕГАТ	FREGAT
FRUIT	ФРУКТ	FRUKT

Kick-start Learning Russian:
2000 RUSSIAN Words You didn't Know You Knew

FUNCTION	ФУНКЦИЯ	FUNKTSIYA
FUND	ФОНД	FOND
FUNDRAISING	ФАНДРАЙЗИНГ	FANDRAYZING
FURUNCLE	ФУРУНКУЛ	FURUNKUL
FUSELAGE	ФЮЗЕЛЯЖ	FYUZELYAZH
FUTURISM	ФУТУРИЗМ	FUTURIZM
FUTURIST	ФУТУРИСТ	FUTURIST

G

ENGLISH	RUSSIAN	PRONONSIATION
GADGET	ГАДЖЕТ	GADZHET
GALAXY	ГАЛАКТИКА	GALAKTIKA
GARLAND	ГИРЛЯНДА	GIRLYANDA
GEISHA	ГЕЙША	GEYSHA
GELATIN	ЖЕЛАТИН	ZHELATIN
GENEALOGY	ГЕНЕАЛОГИЯ	GENEALOGIYA
GENERAL	ГЕНЕРАЛ	GENERAL
GENETICS	ГЕНЕТИКА	GENETIKA
GENRE	ЖАНР	ZHANR
GENTLEMAN	ДЖЕНТЛЬМЕН	DZHENTL'MEN
GEOGRAPHY	ГЕОГРАФИЯ	GEOGRAFIYA
GEOMETRY	ГЕОМЕТРИЯ	GEOMETRIYA
GERANIUM	ГЕРАНЬ	GERAN'
GESTAPO	ГЕСТАПО	GESTAPO
GEYSER	ГЕЙЗЕР	GEYZER
GHETTO	ГЕТТО	GETTO
GIANT	ГИГАНТ	GIGANT

GIBBON	ГИББОН	GIBBON
GIRAFFE	ЖИРАФ	ZHIRAF
GIRLFRIEND	ГЁРЛФРЕНД	GIORLFREND
GLADIATOR	ГЛАДИАТОР	GLADIATOR
GLADIOLUS	ГЛАДИОЛУС	GLADIOLUS
GLAUCOMA	ГЛАУКОМА	GLAUKOMA
GLAZE	ГЛАЗУРЬ	GLAZUR'
GLOBAL	ГЛОБАЛЬНЫЙ	GLOBAL'NYY
GLOBE	ГЛОБУС	GLOBUS
GLUCOSE	ГЛЮКОЗА	GLYUKOZA
GLYCERIN	ГЛИЦЕРИН	GLITSERIN
GOALKEEPER	ГОЛКИПЕР	GOLKIPER
GOLF	ГОЛЬФ	GOL'F
GONDOLA	ГОНДОЛА	GONDOLA
GOOGLE (N)	ГУГЛ	GUGL
GOOGLE (V)	ГУГЛИТЬ	GUGLIT'
GOTHIC	ГОТИКА	GOTIKA
GOUACHE	ГУАШЬ	GUASH'
GPS-TRACKER	GPS-ТРЕКЕР	GPS-TREKER
GRAM	ГРАММ	GRAMM
GRAMMAR	ГРАММАТИКА	GRAMMATIKA
GRANITE	ГРАНИТ	GRANIT

GRANT	ГРАНТ	GRANT
GRAPHICS	ГРАФИКА	GRAFIKA
GRAVITY	ГРАВИТАЦИЯ	GRAVITATSIYA
GROG	ГРОГ	GROG
GROUP	ГРУППА	GRUPPA
GUIDE	ГИД	GID
GUITAR	ГИТАРА	GITARA
GYMNAST	ГИМНАСТ	GIMNAST
GYMNASTICS	ГИМНАСТИКА	GIMNASTIKA
GYPSUM	ГИПС	GIPS

Н

ENGLISH	RUSSIAN	PRONONSIATION
HALL	ХОЛЛ	KHOLL
HALLUCINATION	ГАЛЛЮЦИНАЦИЯ	GALLYUTSINATSIYA
HANDS-FREE	ХЕНДС-ФРИ	KHENDS-FRI
HARD DRIVE	ХАРД-ДРАЙВ	KHARD-DRAYV
HEAD-LINER	ХЕДЛАЙНЕР	KHEDLAYNER
HEMOGLOBIN	ГЕМОГЛОБИН	GEMOGLOBIN
HEMORRHOID	ГЕМОРРОЙ	GEMORROY
HERBICIDE	ГЕРБИЦИД	GERBITSID
HERCULES	ГЕРКУЛЕС	GERKULES
HERO	ГЕРОЙ	GEROY
HEROIN	ГЕРОИН	GEROIN
HEROISM	ГЕРОИЗМ	GEROIZM
HIPPIE	ХИППИ	KHIPPI
HIPPOPOTAMUS	ГИППОПОТАМ	GIPPOPOTAM
HISTORY	ИСТОРИЯ	ISTORIYA
HOBBY	ХОББИ	KHOBBI
HOCKEY	ХОККЕЙ	KHOKKEY

HOLOGRAM	ГОЛОГРАММА	GOLOGRAMMA
HOMEOPATHY	ГОМЕОПАТИЯ	GOMEOPATIYA
HOMOSEXUALITY	ГОМОСЕКСУАЛИЗМ	GOMOSEKSUALIZM
HORIZON	ГОРИЗОНТ	GORIZONT
HOSPITAL	ГОСПИТАЛЬ	GOSPITAL'
HUMANISM	ГУМАНИЗМ	GUMANIZM
HUMOR	ЮМОР	YUMOR
HYACINTH	ГИАЦИНТ	GIATSINT
HYBRID	ГИБРИД	GIBRID
HYDRAULICS	ГИДРАВЛИКА	GIDRAVLIKA
HYENA	ГИЕНА	GIYENA
HYGIENE	ГИГИЕНА	GIGIYENA
HYPERBOLE	ГИПЕРБОЛА	GIPERBOLA
HYPOTENUSE	ГИПОТЕНУЗА	GIPOTENUZA
HYPOTHESIS	ГИПОТЕЗА	GIPOTEZA
HYSTERIA	ИСТЕРИЯ	ISTERIYA
HYSTERICS	ИСТЕРИКА	ISTERIKA

I

ENGLISH	RUSSIAN	PRONONSIATION
ICON	ИКОНА	IKONA
IDEA	ИДЕЯ	IDEYA
IDEAL	ИДЕАЛ	IDEAL
IDEALISM	ИДЕАЛИЗМ	IDEALIZM
IDENTICAL	ИДЕНТИЧНЫЙ	IDENTICHNYY
IDEOLOGY	ИДЕОЛОГИЯ	IDEOLOGIYA
IDIOM	ИДИОМА	IDIOMA
IDIOT	ИДИОТ	IDIOT
IDOL	ИДОЛ	IDOL
ILLUMINATION	ИЛЛЮМИНАЦИЯ	ILLYUMINATSIYA
ILLUMINATOR	ИЛЛЮМИНАТОР	ILLYUMINATOR
ILLUSION	ИЛЛЮЗИЯ	ILLYUZIYA
ILLUSTRATION	ИЛЛЮСТРАЦИЯ	ILLYUSTRATSIYA
ILLUSTRATOR	ИЛЛЮСТРАТОР	ILLYUSTRATOR
IMAGE	ИМИДЖ	IMIDZH
IMITATION	ИМИТАЦИЯ	IMITATSIYA
IMMIGRANT	ИММИГРАНТ	IMMIGRANT

IMMUNITY	ИММУНИТЕТ	IMMUNITET
IMMUNOLOGY	ИММУНОЛОГИЯ	IMMUNOLOGIYA
IMPEACHMENT	ИМПИЧМЕНТ	IMPICHMENT
IMPERATOR	ИМПЕРАТОР	IMPERATOR
IMPERIA	ИМПЕРИЯ	IMPERIYA
IMPLANT	ИМПЛАНТ	IMPLANT
IMPORT	ИМПОРТ	IMPORT
IMPRESSIONISM	ИМПРЕССИОНИЗМ	IMPRESSIONIZM
IMPRESSIONIST	ИМПРЕССИОНИСТ	IMPRESSIONIST
IMPROVISATION	ИМПРОВИЗАЦИЯ	IMPROVIZATSIYA
IMPULSE	ИМПУЛЬС	IMPUL'S
INCIDENT	ИНЦИДЕНТ	INTSIDENT
INCUBATION	ИНКУБАЦИЯ	INKUBATSIYA
INCUBATOR	ИНКУБАТОР	INKUBATOR
INDEX	ИНДЕКС	INDEKS
INDEXING	ИНДЕКСАЦИЯ	INDEKSATSIYA
INDICATOR	ИНДИКАТОР	INDIKATOR
INDIGO	ИНДИГО	INDIGO
INDIVIDUAL	ИНДИВИДУАЛ	INDIVIDUAL
INDIVIDUALIST	ИНДИВИДУАЛИСТ	INDIVIDUALIST
INDUCTION	ИНДУКЦИЯ	INDUKTSIYA
INDUCTOR	ИНДУКТОР	INDUKTOR

INDUSTRY	ИНДУСТРИЯ	INDUSTRIYA
INERTIA	ИНЕРЦИЯ	INERTSIYA
INFECTION	ИНФЕКЦИЯ	INFEKTSIYA
INFINITIVE	ИНФИНИТИВ	INFINITIV
INFLATION	ИНФЛЯЦИЯ	INFLYATSIYA
INFOGRAPHICS	ИНФОГРАФИКА	INFOGRAFIKA
INFORMATICS	ИНФОРМАТИКА	INFORMATIKA
INFORMATION	ИНФОРМАЦИЯ	INFORMATSIYA
INGREDIENT	ИНГРЕДИЕНТ	INGREDIYENT
INHALATION	ИНГАЛЯЦИЯ	INGALYATSIYA
INHALER	ИНГАЛЯТОР	INGALYATOR
INITIATOR	ИНИЦИАТОР	INITSIATOR
INJECTION	ИНЪЕКЦИЯ	IN"YEKTSIYA
INNOVATION	ИННОВАЦИЯ	INNOVATSIYA
INPOTENT	ИМПОТЕНТ	IMPOTENT
INQUISITOR	ИНКВИЗИТОР	INKVIZITOR
INSPECTION	ИНСПЕКЦИЯ	INSPEKTSIYA
INSPECTOR	ИНСПЕКТОР	INSPEKTOR
INSTINCT	ИНСТИНКТ	INSTINKT
INSTITUTE	ИНСТИТУТ	INSTITUT
INSTRUCTION	ИНСТРУКЦИЯ	INSTRUKTSIYA
INSTRUCTOR	ИНСТРУКТОР	INSTRUKTOR
INSTRUMENT	ИНСТРУМЕНТ	INSTRUMENT

INSULIN	ИНСУЛИН	INSULIN
INTEGRAL	ИНТЕГРАЛ	INTEGRAL
INTELLECT	ИНТЕЛЛЕКТ	INTELLEKT
INTELLECTUAL	ИНТЕЛЛЕКТУАЛ	INTELLEKTUAL
INTERACTIVE	ИНТЕРАКТИВ	INTERAKTIV
INTEREST	ИНТЕРЕС	INTERES
INTERFACE	ИНТЕРФЕЙС	INTERFEYS
INTERIOR	ИНТЕРЬЕР	INTER'YER
INTERN	ИНТЕРН	INTERN
INTERNACIONALIST	ИНТЕРНАЦИОНАЛИСТ	INTERNATSIONALIST
INTERNATIONAL	ИНТЕРНАЦИОНАЛ	INTERNATSIONAL
INTERNATIONALISM	ИНТЕРНАЦИОНАЛИЗМ	INTERNATSIONALIZM
INTERNET	ИНТЕРНЕТ	INTERNET
INTERPOL	ИНТЕРПОЛ	INTERPOL
INTERPRETER	ИНТЕРПРЕТАТОР	INTERPRETATOR
INTERVAL	ИНТЕРВАЛ	INTERVAL
INTERVIEW	ИНТЕРВЬЮ	INTERV'YU
INTONATION	ИНТОНАЦИЯ	INTONATSIYA
INTOXICATION	ИНТОКСИКАЦИЯ	INTOKSIKATSIYA
INTRIGUE	ИНТРИГА	INTRIGA
INTUITION	ИНТУИЦИЯ	INTUITSIYA
INVALID	ИНВАЛИД	INVALID

INVERSION	ИНВЕРСИЯ	INVERSIYA
INVESTMENT	ИНВЕСТИЦИЯ	INVESTITSIYA
ION	ЙОН	ION
IRONY	ИРОНИЯ	IRONIYA
IRRADIATION	ИРРАДИАЦИЯ	IRRADIATSIYA
IRRIGATION	ИРРИГАЦИЯ	IRRIGATSIYA
ISOLATOR	ИЗОЛЯТОР	IZOLYATOR
ISOTOPE	ИЗОТОП	IZOTOP

J

ENGLISH	RUSSIAN	PRONONSIATION
JAM	ДЖЕМ	DZHEM
JASMINE	ЖАСМИН	ZHASMIN
JAZZ	ДЖАЗ	DZHAZ
JEANS	ДЖИНСЫ	DZHINSY
JEEP	ДЖИП	DZHIP
JIU-JITSU	ДЖИУ-ДЖИТСУ	DZHIU-DZHITSU
JUDO	ДЗЮДО	DZYUDO
JUMPER	ДЖЕМПЕР	DZHEMPER
JUNGLE	ДЖУНГЛИ	DZHUNGLI
JUNIOR	ЮНИОР	YUNIOR
JUNTA	ХУНТА	KHUNTA
JURY	ЖЮРИ	ZHYURI

Kick-start Learning Russian:
2000 RUSSIAN Words You didn't Know You Knew

K

ENGLISH	RUSSIAN	PRONONSIATION
KALEIDOSCOPE	КАЛЕЙДОСКОП	KALEYDOSKOP
KANGAROO	КЕНГУРУ	KENGURU
KAOLIN	КАОЛИН	KAOLIN
KARATE	КАРАТЭ	KARATE
KART	КАРТ	KART
KEROSENE	КЕРОСИН	КЕРОСИН
KICKBOXING	КИКБОКСИНГ	KIKBOKSING
KILLER	КИЛЛЕР	KILLER
KILOMETER	КИЛОМЕТР	KILOMETR
KILOWATT	КИЛОВАТТ	KILOVATT
KIMONO	КИМОНО	KIMONO
KINEMATICS	КИНЕМАТИКА	KINEMATIKA
KIOSK	КИОСК	KIOSK
KOMSOMOL	КОМСОМОЛ	KOMSOMOL
KORRIDA	КОРРИДА	KORRIDA

Kick-start Learning Russian:
2000 RUSSIAN Words You didn't Know You Knew

L

ENGLISH	RUSSIAN	PRONONSIATION
LABORATORY	ЛАБОРАТОРИЯ	LABORATORIYA
LAGOON	ЛАГУНА	LAGUNA
LAMP	ЛАМПА	LAMPA
LAVENDER	ЛАВАНДА	LAVANDA
LEADER	ЛИДЕР	LIDER
LEASING	ЛИЗИНГ	LIZING
LECTURE	ЛЕКЦИЯ	LEKTSIYA
LECTURER	ЛЕКТОР	LEKTOR
LEGEND	ЛЕГЕНДА	LEGENDA
LEMON	ЛИМОН	LIMON
LEMONADE	ЛИМОНАД	LIMONAD
LENS	ЛИНЗА	LINZA
LETHARGY	ЛЕТАРГИЯ	LETARGIYA
LEUCOCYTES	ЛЕЙКОЦИТЫ	LEYKOTSITY
LEXICON	ЛЕКСИКОН	LEKSIKON
LIBERAL	ЛИБЕРАЛ	LIBERAL
LIBERALISM	ЛИБЕРАЛИЗМ	LIBERALIZM

LIBRETTO	ЛИБРЕТТО	ЛИБРЕ**TT**О
LIEUTENANT	ЛЕЙТЕНАНТ	LEYTE**N**A**N**T
LIFT	ЛИФТ	LI**F**T
LIQUIDATOR	ЛИКВИДАТОР	LIKVID**A**TOR
LILLIPUT	ЛИЛИПУТ	LILIP**UT**
LILY	ЛИЛИЯ	LIL**I**YA
LIMIT	ЛИМИТ	LIM**I**T
LIMOUSINE	ЛИМУЗИН	LIMUZI**N**
LINE	ЛИНИЯ	L**I**NIYA
LINGUIST	ЛИНГВИСТ	LINGV**I**ST
LINGUISTICS	ЛИНГВИСТИКА	LINGV**I**ST**I**KA
LINOLEUM	ЛИНОЛЕУМ	LIN**O**LEUM
LIQUIDATION	ЛИКВИДАЦИЯ	LIKVID**A**TSIYA
LITERATURE	ЛИТЕРАТУРА	LITERA**TU**RA
LITHOGRAPHY	ЛИТОГРАФИЯ	LITOGRA**FI**YA
LITRE	ЛИТР	LI**T**R
LOCATOR	ЛОКАТОР	LOK**A**TOR
LOGIC	ЛОГИКА	LOG**I**KA
LOGISTICS	ЛОГИСТИКА	LOG**I**ST**I**KA
LORD	ЛОРД	L**O**RD
LOTION	ЛОСЬОН	LOS**'O**N
LOTTERY	ЛОТЕРЕЯ	LOTE**RE**YA

LOTTO	ΛΟΤΟ	LOT**O**
LOTUS	ΛΟΤΟΣ	L**O**TOS
LOW COST	ΛΟΥΚΟΣΤ	LOUK**O**ST

Kick-start Learning Russian:
2000 RUSSIAN Words You didn't Know You Knew

M

ENGLISH	RUSSIAN	PRONONSIATION
MACRAME	МАКРАМЕ	MAKRAME
MADAME	МАДАМ	MADAM
MADONNA	МАДОННА	MADONNA
MAESTRO	МАЭСТРО	MAESTRO
MAFIA	МАФИЯ	MAFIYA
MAGIC	МАГИЯ	MAGIYA
MAGNET	МАГНИТ	MAGNIT
MAGNETISM	МАГНЕТИЗМ	MAGNETIZM
MANGO	МАНГО	MAHGO
MALARIA	МАЛЯРИЯ	MALYARIYA
MANAGEMENT	МЕНЕДЖМЕНТ	MENEDZHMENT
MANAGER	МЕНЕДЖЕР	MENEDZHER
MANDARIN	МАНДАРИН	MANDARIN
MANIA	МАНИЯ	MANIYA
MANIFESTO	МАНИФЕСТ	MANIFEST
MANIPULATOR	МАНИПУЛЯТОР	MANIPULYATOR

MANNEQUIN	МАНЕКЕН	MANEKEN
MANTLE	МАНТИЯ	MANTIYA
MANUFACTURE	МАНУФАКТУРА	MANUFAKTURA
MANUSCRIPT	МАНУСКРИПТ	MANUSKRIPT
MARATHON	МАРАФОН	MARAFON
MARGARINE	МАРГАРИН	MARGARIN
MARIJUANA	МАРИХУАНА	MARIKHUANA
MARINADE	МАРИНАД	MARINAD
MARKET	МАРКЕТ	MARKET
MARKETING	МАРКЕТИНГ	MARKETING
MARXISM	МАРКСИЗМ	MARKSIZM
MASSAGE	МАССАЖ	MASSAZH
MASTIC	МАСТИКА	MASTIKA
MATADOR	МАТАДОР	MATADOR
MATERIAL	МАТЕРИАЛ	MATERIAL
MATHEMATICS	МАТЕМАТИКА	MATEMATIKA
MAUSER	МАУЗЕР	MAUZER
MAUSOLEUM	МАВЗОЛЕЙ	MAVZOLEY
MAXIMUM	МАКСИМУМ	MAKSIMUM
MAYONNAISE	МАЙОНЕЗ	MAYONE3
MAYOR	МЭР	MER
MECHANIC	МЕХАНИК	MEKHANIK

MECHANICS	МЕХАНИКА	MEKHANIKA
MECHANISM	МЕХАНИЗМ	MEKHANIZM
MEDAL	МЕДАЛЬ	MEDAL'
MEDALLION	МЕДАЛЬОН	MEDAL'ON
MEDIAN	МЕДИАНА	MEDIANA
MEDICINE	МЕДИЦИНА	MEDITSINA
MEDITATION	МЕДИТАЦИЯ	MEDITATSIYA
MEETING	МИТИНГ	MITING
MEGAPOLIS	МЕГАПОЛИС	MEGAPOLIS
MELANCHOLY	МЕЛАНХОЛИЯ	MELANKHOLIYA
MELODY	МЕЛОДИЯ	MELODIYA
MEMBRANE	МЕМБРАНА	MEMBRANA
MEMORANDUM	МЕМОРАНДУМ	MEMORANDUM
MEMORIAL	МЕМОРИАЛ	MEMORIAL
MENINGITIS	МЕНИНГИТ	MENINGIT
MENTHOL	МЕНТОЛ	MENTOL
MERIDIAN	МЕРИДИАН	MERIDIAN
MESSAGE	МЕССЕДЖ	MESSEDZH
METAL	МЕТАЛЛ	METALL
METAMORPHOSIS	МЕТАМОРФОЗА	METAMORFOZA
METAPHOR	МЕТАФОРА	METAFORA
METAPHYSICIAN	МЕТАФИЗИК	METAFIZIK
METAPHYSICS	МЕТАФИЗИКА	METAFIZIKA

METEORITE	МЕТЕОРИТ	METEOR**I**T
METEOROLOGIST	МЕТЕОРОЛОГ	METEOR**O**LOG
METEOROLOGY	МЕТЕОРОЛОГИЯ	METEOROL**O**GIYA
METER	МЕТР	M**E**TR
METHOD	МЕТОД	M**E**TOD
MEZZANINE	МЕЗОНИН	MEZON**I**N
MEZZO-SOPRANO	МЕЦЦО-СОПРАНО	M**E**TS**T**SO-SOP**RA**NO
MICROBE	МИКРОБ	MIKR**O**B
MICROBIOLOGIST	МИКРОБИОЛОГ	MIKROB**I**OLOG
MICROCLIMATE	МИКРОКЛИМАТ	MIKROKL**I**MAT
MICROMETER	МИКРОМЕТР	MIKR**O**METR
MICRON	МИКРОН	MIKR**O**N
MICROORGANISM	МИКРООРГАНИЗМ	MIKROORGAN**I**ZM
MICROPHONE	МИКРОФОН	MIKROF**O**N
MICROPROCESSOR	МИКРОПРОЦЕССОР	MIKROPROTS**E**SSOR
MICROSCOPE	МИКРОСКОП	MIKROSK**O**P
MIGRAINE	МИГРЕНЬ	MIGR**E**N'
MIGRATION	МИГРАЦИЯ	MIGR**A**TSIYA
MILITARISM	МИЛИТАРИЗМ	MILITAR**I**ZM
MILLIMETER	МИЛЛИМЕТР	MILLIM**E**TR
MILLION	МИЛЛИОН	MILL**I**ON
MILLIONAIRE	МИЛЛИОНЕР	MILLION**E**R

MILORD	МИЛОРД	MIL**O**RD
MIMOSA	МИМОЗА	MIM**O**ZA
MINERAL	МИНЕРАЛ	MINER**A**L
MINERALOGY	МИНЕРАЛОГИЯ	MINERAL**O**GIYA
MINIATURE	МИНИАТЮРА	MINIAT**YU**RA
MINIMUM	МИНИМУМ	M**I**NIMUM
MINISTER	МИНИСТР	MIN**I**STR
MINUET	МЕНУЭТ	MENU**E**T
MINUS	МИНУС	M**I**NUS
MINUTE	МИНУТА	MIN**U**TA
MIRAGE	МИРАЖ	MIR**A**ZH
MISS/ MISSIS	МИСС/ МИССИС	M**I**SS/ M**I**SSIS
MISSION	МИССИЯ	M**I**SSIYA
MISTER	МИСТЕР	M**I**STER
MOBILIZATION	МОБИЛИЗАЦИЯ	MOBILIZ**A**TSIYA
MODEL	МОДЕЛЬ	MOD**E**L'
MODERN	МОДЕРН	MOD**E**RN
MODULE	МОДУЛЬ	M**O**DUL'
MOLECULE	МОЛЕКУЛА	MOL**E**KULA
MOLLUSK	МОЛЛЮСК	MOLL**YU**SK
MONITOR	МОНИТОР	MONIT**O**R
MONOGRAPH	МОНОГРАФИЯ	MONOGR**A**FIYA
MONOLOGUE	МОНОЛОГ	MONOL**O**G

MONOPOLIST	МОНОПОЛИСТ	MONOPOLIST
MONOPOLY	МОНОПОЛИЯ	MONOPOLIYA
MONOTYPE	МОНОТИП	MONOTIP
MONSTER	МОНСТР	MONSTR
MONUMENT	МОНУМЕНТ	MONUMENT
MORAL	МОРАЛЬ	MORAL'
MORATORIUM	МОРАТОРИЙ	MORATORIY
MORGUE	МОРГ	MORG
MORPHINE	МОРФИЙ	MORFIY
MORPHOLOGY	МОРФОЛОГИЯ	MORFOLOGIYA
MOSAIC	МОЗАИКА	MOZAIKA
MOSQUITO	МОСКИТ	MOSKIT
MOTEL	МОТЕЛЬ	MOTEL'
MOTIVE	МОТИВ	MOTIV
MOTOBALL	МОТОБОЛ	MOTOBOL
MOTORCYCLE	МОТОЦИКЛ	MOTOTSIKL
MOTORCYCLIST	МОТОЦИКЛИСТ	MOTOTSIKLIST
MOUSSE	МУСС	MUSS
MUMMY	МУМИЯ	MUMIYA
MUNICIPALITY	МУНИЦИПАЛИТЕТ	MUNITSIPALITET
MUNICIPALIZATION	МУНИЦИПАЛИЗАЦИЯ	MUNITSIPALIZATSIYA
MUSCAT	МУСКАТ	MUSKAT

MUSCLE	МУСКУЛ	MUSKUL
MUSEUM	МУЗЕЙ	MUZEY
MUSIC	МУЗЫКА	MUZYKA
MUSICAL	МЮЗИКЛ	MYUZIKL
MUSICIAN	МУЗЫКАНТ	MUZYKANT
MUSKETEER	МУШКЕТЁР	MUSHKETOR
MUSTANG	МУСТАНГ	MUSTANG
MUTANT	МУТАНТ	MUTANT
MUTATION	МУТАЦИЯ	MUTATSIYA
MYSTICISM	МИСТИЦИЗМ	MISTITSIZM
MYSTIFICATION	МИСТИФИКАЦИЯ	MISTIFIKATSIYA

Kick-start Learning Russian:
2000 RUSSIAN Words You didn't Know You Knew

N

ENGLISH	RUSSIAN	PRONONSIATION
NAIVETY	НАИВНОСТЬ	NAIVNOST'
NANNY	НЯНЯ	NYANYA
NARCISSUS	НАРЦИСС	NARTSISS
NARCOLOGY	НАРКОЛОГИЯ	NARKOLOGIYA
NATION	НАЦИЯ	NATSIYA
NATIONALISM	НАЦИОНАЛИЗМ	NATSIONALIZM
NATIONALIST	НАЦИОНАЛИСТ	NATSIONALIST
NATIONALITY	НАЦИОНАЛЬНОСТЬ	NATSIONAL'NOST'
NATIONALIZATION	НАЦИОНАЛИЗАЦИЯ	NATSIONALIZATSIYA
NATURALISM	НАТУРАЛИЗМ	NATURALIZM
NATURALIST	НАТУРАЛИСТ	NATURALIST
NAVIGATION	НАВИГАЦИЯ	NAVIGATSIYA
NAZISM	НАЦИЗМ	NATSIZM
NEGATIVE	НЕГАТИВ	NEGATIV
NEGATIVISM	НЕГАТИВИЗМ	NEGATIVIZM
NERVE	НЕРВ	NERV
NEUROLOGIST	НЕВРОЛОГ	NEVROLOG

NEUROLOGY	НЕВРОЛОГИЯ	NEVROLOGIYA
NEURON	НЕЙРОН	NEYRON
NEUTRALITY	НЕЙТРАЛИТЕТ	NEYTRALITET
NEUTRON	НЕЙТРОН	NEYTRON
NEWS MAKER	НЬЮСМЕЙКЕР	N'YUSMEYKER
NEWSROOM	НЬЮСРУМ	N'YUSRUM
NOCTURNE	НОКТЮРН	NOKTYURN
NOSE	НОС	NOS
NOVOCAINE	НОВОКАИН	NOVOKAIN
NUANCE	НЮАНС	NYUANS
NUDISM	НУДИЗМ	NUDIZM
NUDIST	НУДИСТ	NUDIST
NUMISMATICS	НУМИЗМАТИКА	NUMIZMATIKA
NYMPH	НИМФА	NIMFA

O

ENGLISH	RUSSIAN	PRONONSIATION
OBJECT	ОБЪЕКТ	OB"YEKT
OCEAN	ОКЕАН	OKEAH
OCEANOLOGY	ОКЕАНОЛОГИЯ	OKEANOLOGIYA
OCULAR	ОКУЛЯР	OKULYAR
OFFICE	ОФИС	OFIS
OFFICER	ОФИЦЕР	OFITSER
OFFLINE	ОФЛАЙН	OFLAYN
OLEANDER	ОЛЕАНДР	OLEANDR
OLIVE	ОЛИВА	OLIVA
OLYMPICS	ОЛИМПИАДА	OLIMPIADA
OLYMPUS	ОЛИМП	OLIMP
ONCOLOGY	ОНКОЛОГИЯ	ONKOLOGIYA
OPAL	ОПАЛ	OPAL
OPHTHALMOLOGY	ОФТАЛЬМОЛОГИЯ	OFTAL'MOLOGIYA
OPPONENT	ОППОНЕНТ	OPPONENT
OPTICS	ОПТИКА	OPTIKA
OPTIMISM	ОПТИМИЗМ	OPTIMIZM

OPTIMIST	ОПТИМИСТ	OPTIMIST
ORBIT	ОРБИТА	ORBITA
ORCHESTRA	ОРКЕСТР	OPKECTP
ORCHID	ОРХИДЕЯ	ORKHIDEYA
ORGANISM	ОРГАНИЗМ	ORGANIZM
ORGANIST	ОРГАНИСТ	ORGANIST
ORGANIZATION	ОРГАНИЗАЦИЯ	ORGANIZATSIYA
ORGASM	ОРГАЗМ	ORGAZM
ORGY	ОРГИЯ	ORGIYA
ORIGINAL	ОРИГИНАЛ	ORIGINAL
ORTHOGRAPHY	ОРФОГРАФИЯ	ORFOGRAFIYA
ORTHOPEDICS	ОРТОПЕДИЯ	ORTOPEDIYA
OTOLARYNGOLOGY	ОТОЛАРИНГОЛОГИЯ	OTOLARINGOLOGIYA
OUTLET	АУТЛЕТ	AUTLET

P

ENGLISH	RUSSIAN	PRONONSIATION
PACIFISM	ПАЦИФИЗМ	PATSIFIZM
PACIFIST	ПАЦИФИСТ	PATSIFIST
PAEDIATRICS	ПЕДИАТРИЯ	PEDIATRIYA
PAGER	ПЕЙДЖЕР	PEYDZHER
PAJAMAS	ПИЖАМА	PIZHAMA
PALEOGRAPHY	ПАЛЕОГРАФИЯ	PALEOGRAFIYA
PALEONTOLOGY	ПАЛЕОНТОЛОГИЯ	PALEONTOLOGIYA
PANIC	ПАНИКА	PANIKA
PANORAMA	ПАНОРАМА	PANORAMA
PAPHOS	ПАФОС	PAFOS
PAPIER-MACHE	ПАПЬЕ-МАШЕ	PAP'YE-MASHE
PAPYRUS	ПАПИРУС	PAPIRUS
PARABOLA	ПАРАБОЛА	PARABOLA
PARACHUTE	ПАРАШЮТ	PARASHYUT
PARADOX	ПАРАДОКС	PARADOKS
PARAFFIN	ПАРАФИН	PARAFIN
PARAGRAPH	ПАРАГРАФ	PARAGRAF

PARALLEL	ПАРАЛЛЕЛЬ	PARALLEL'
PARALLELEPIPED	ПАРАЛЛЕЛЕПИПЕД	PARALLELEPIPED
PARALLELOGRAM	ПАРАЛЛЕЛОГРАММ	PARALLELOGRAMM
PARALYSIS	ПАРАЛИЧ	PARALICH
PARAMETER	ПАРАМЕТР	PARAMETR
PARANOIA	ПАРАНОЙЯ	PARANOYYA
PARAPSYCHOLOGY	ПАРАПСИХОЛОГИЯ	PARAPSIKHOLOGIYA
PARASITE	ПАРАЗИТ	PARAZIT
PARITY	ПАРИТЕТ	PARITET
PARK	ПАРК	PARK
PARKING	ПАРКИНГ	PARKING
PARLIAMENT	ПАРЛАМЕНТ	PARLAMENT
PARLIAMENTARISM	ПАРЛАМЕНТАРИЗМ	PARLAMENTARIZM
PARODY	ПАРОДИЯ	PARODIYA
PAROLE	ПАРОЛЬ	PAROL'
PARQUET	ПАРКЕТ	PARKET
PARTIZAN	ПАРТИЗАН	PARTIZAN
PARTY	ПАРТИЯ	PARTIYA
PASSENGER	ПАССАЖИР	PASSAZHIR
PASSIVE	ПАССИВ	PASSIV
PASSPORT	ПАСПОРТ	PASPORT
PASTE	ПАСТА	PASTA

PASTEL	ПАСТЕЛЬ	PASTEL'
PASTOR	ПАСТОР	PASTOR
PATENT	ПАТЕНТ	PATENT
PATHOLOGY	ПАТОЛОГИЯ	PATOLOGIYA
PATIENT	ПАЦИЕНТ	PATSIYENT
PATRIARCH	ПАТРИАРХ	PATRIARKH
PATRIOT	ПАТРИОТ	PATRIOT
PATROL	ПАТРУЛЬ	PATRUL'
PAUSE	ПАУЗА	PAUZA
PAVILION	ПАВИЛЬОН	PAVIL'ON
PEARL	ПЕРЛ	PERL
PEDAL	ПЕДАЛЬ	PEDAL'
PEDANTISM	ПЕДАНТИЗМ	PEDANTIZM
PEDESTAL	ПЬЕДЕСТАЛ	P'YEDESTAL
PEDICURE	ПЕДИКЮР	PEDIKYUR
PELICAN	ПЕЛИКАН	PELIKAN
PENALTY	ПЕНАЛЬТИ	PENAL'TI
PENGUIN	ПИНГВИН	PINGVIN
PENICILLIN	ПЕНИЦИЛЛИН	PENITSILLIN
PENNY	ПЕННИ	PENNI
PENSION	ПЕНСИЯ	PENSIYA
PENSIONER	ПЕНСИОНЕР	PENSIONER
PENTHOUSE	ПЕНТХАУС	PENTKHAUS

PERCENT	ПРОЦЕНТ	PROTSENT
PERFORATOR	ПЕРФОРАТОР	PERFORATOR
PERFUMERY	ПАРФЮМЕРИЯ	PARFYUMERIYA
PERIOD	ПЕРИОД	PERIOD
PERIODICALS	ПЕРИОДИКА	PERIODIKA
PERIPHERY	ПЕРИФЕРИЯ	PERIFERIYA
PERITONITIS	ПЕРИТОНИТ	PERITONIT
PERPENDICULAR	ПЕРПЕНДИКУЛЯР	PERPENDIKULYAR
PERSON	ПЕРСОНА	PERSONA
PERSONAGE	ПЕРСОНАЖ	PERSONAZH
PERSONNEL	ПЕРСОНАЛ	PERSONAL
PERSPECTIVE	ПЕРСПЕКТИВА	PERSPEKTIVA
PESSIMISM	ПЕССИМИЗМ	PESSIMIZM
PESSIMIST	ПЕССИМИСТ	PESSIMIST
PETITION	ПЕТИЦИЯ	PETITSIYA
PHANTOM	ФАНТОМ	FANTOM
PHARAOH	ФАРАОН	FARAON
PHARMACOLOGY	ФАРМАКОЛОГИЯ	FARMAKOLOGIYA
PHASE	ФАЗА	FAZA
PHENOMENON	ФЕНОМЕН	FENOMEN
PHILANTHROPIST	ФИЛАНТРОП	FILANTROP
PHILATELY	ФИЛАТЕЛИЯ	FILATELIYA

PHILOSOPHER	ФИЛОСОФ	FILOSOF
PHILOSOPHY	ФИЛОСОФИЯ	FILOSOFIYA
PHONETICS	ФОНЕТИКА	FONETIKA
PHONOGRAM	ФОНОГРАММА	FONOGRAMMA
PHOTO	ФОТО	FOTO
PHOTOCHRONICLE	ФОТОХРОНИКА	FOTOKHRONIKA
PHOTOSET	ФОТОСЕТ	FOTOSET
PHOTOSYNTHESIS	ФОТОСИНТЕЗ	FOTOSINTEZ
PHRASE	ФРАЗА	FRAZA
PHRASEOLOGY	ФРАЗЕОЛОГИЯ	FRAZEOLOGIYA
PHYSICS	ФИЗИКА	FIZIKA
PHYSIOLOGY	ФИЗИОЛОГИЯ	FIZIOLOGIYA
PHYSIOTHERAPIST	ФИЗИОТЕРАПЕВТ	FIZIOTERAPEVT
PHYSIOTHERAPY	ФИЗИОТЕРАПИЯ	FIZIOTERAPIYA
PIANO, PIANINO	ПИАНИНО	PIANINO
PICNIC	ПИКНИК	PIKNIK
PIGMENT	ПИГМЕНТ	PIGMENT
PILGRIM	ПИЛИГРИМ	PILIGRIM
PILOT	ПИЛОТ	PILOT
PINTA	ПИНТА	PINTA
PIONEER	ПИОНЕР	PIONER
PIPETTE	ПИПЕТКА	PIPETKA
PIRATE	ПИРАТ	PIRAT

Kick-start Learning Russian:
2000 RUSSIAN Words You didn't Know You Knew

PIROUETTE	ПИРУЭТ	PIRUET
PISTOL	ПИСТОЛЕТ	PISTOLET
PISTONE	ПИСТОН	PISTON
PLACENTA	ПЛАЦЕНТА	PLATSENTA
PLAGIARISM	ПЛАГИАТ	PLAGIAT
PLAID	ПЛЕД	PLED
PLAN	ПЛАН	PLAN
PLANET	ПЛАНЕТА	PLANETA
PLANKTON	ПЛАНКТОН	PLANKTON
PLANTATION	ПЛАНТАЦИЯ	PLANTATSIYA
PLASTICINE	ПЛАСТИЛИН	PLASTILIN
PLATFORM	ПЛАТФОРМА	PLATFORMA
PLAYER	ПЛЕЕР	PLEER
PLEXIGLASS	ПЛЕКСИГЛАС	PLEKSIGLAS
PLURALISM	ПЛЮРАЛИЗМ	PLYURALIZM
PLUS	ПЛЮС	PLYUS
PNEUMATIC	ПНЕВМАТИКА	PNEVMATIKA
PNEUMONIA	ПНЕВМОНИЯ	PNEVMONIYA
PODIUM	ПОДИУМ	PODIUM
POEM	ПОЭМА	POEMA
POET	ПОЭТ	POET
POETICS	ПОЭТИКА	POETIKA

POETRY	ПОЭЗИЯ	POEZIYA
POLE	ПОЛЮС	POLYUS
POLEMIC	ПОЛЕМИКА	POLEMIKA
POLICE	ПОЛИЦИЯ	POLITSIYA
POLICEMAN	ПОЛИСМЕН	POLISMEN
POLITICS	ПОЛИТИКА	POLITIKA
POLO	ПОЛО	POLO
POLYETHYLENE	ПОЛИЭТИЛЕН	POLIETILEN
POLYGAMY	ПОЛИГАМИЯ	POLIGAMIYA
POLYGLOT	ПОЛИГЛОТ	POLIGLOT
POLYGRAPHY	ПОЛИГРАФИЯ	POLIGRAFIYA
PORNOGRAPHY	ПОРНОГРАФИЯ	PORNOGRAFIYA
PORT	ПОРТ	PORT
PORT WINE	ПОРТВЕЙН	PORTVEYN
PORTAL	ПОРТАЛ	PORTAL
PORTER	ПОРТЬЕ	PORT'YE
PORTION	ПОРЦИЯ	PORTSIYA
PORTRAIT	ПОРТРЕТ	PORTRET
POSE	ПОЗА	POZA
POSITION	ПОЗИЦИЯ	POZITSIYA
POSITIVISM	ПОЗИТИВИЗМ	POZITIVIZM
POSITRON	ПОЗИТРОН	POZITRON
POTENCY	ПОТЕНЦИЯ	POTENTSIYA

POTENTIAL	ПОТЕНЦИАЛ	POTENTSIAL
PRACTICE	ПРАКТИКА	PRAKTIKA
PRAGMATICS	ПРАГМАТИКА	PRAGMATIKA
PRECEDENT	ПРЕЦЕДЕНТ	PRETSEDENT
PREFECTURE	ПРЕФЕКТУРА	PREFEKTURA
PRELUDE	ПРЕЛЮДИЯ	PRELYUDIYA
PREMIERE	ПРЕМЬЕРА	PREM'YERA
PRESENT	ПРЕЗЕНТ	PREZENT
PRESENTATION	ПРЕЗЕНТАЦИЯ	PREZENTATSIYA
PRESIDENT	ПРЕЗИДЕНТ	PREZIDENT
PRESS	ПРЕСС	PRESS
PRESS CONFERENCE	ПРЕСС-КОНФЕРЕНЦИЯ	PRESS-KONFERENTSIYA
PRESTIGE	ПРЕСТИЖ	PRESTIZH
PRESUMPTION	ПРЕЗУМПЦИЯ	PREZUMPTSIYA
PRIMADONNA	ПРИМАДОННА	PRIMADONNA
PRIME MINISTER	ПРЕМЬЕР-МИНИСТР	PREM'YER-MINISTR
PRIMUS	ПРИМУС	PRIMUS
PRINCE	ПРИНЦ	PRINTS
PRINCIPLE	ПРИНЦИП	PRINTSIP
PRINTER	ПРИНТЕР	PRINTER
PRIORITY	ПРИОРИТЕТ	PRIORITET

PRISM	ПРИЗМА	PRIZMA
PRIZE	ПРИЗ	PRIZ
PROBLEM	ПРОБЛЕМА	PROBLEMA
PROCEDURE	ПРОЦЕДУРА	PROTSEDURA
PROCESS	ПРОЦЕСС	PROTSESS
PROCESSOR	ПРОЦЕССОР	PROTSESSOR
PRODUCT	ПРОДУКТ	PRODUKT
PRODUCTION	ПРОИЗВОДСТВО	PROIZVODSTVO
PROFESSION	ПРОФЕССИЯ	PROFESSIYA
PROFESSIONAL	ПРОФЕССИОНАЛ	PROFESSIONAL
PROFESSIONALISM	ПРОФЕССИОНАЛИЗМ	PROFESSIONALIZM
PROFESSOR	ПРОФЕССОР	PROFESSOR
PROFILE	ПРОФИЛЬ	PROFIL'
PROFIT	ПРОФИТ	PROFIT
PROGNOSIS	ПРОГНОЗ	PROGNOZ
PROGRAM	ПРОГРАММА	PROGRAMMA
PROGRAMMER	ПРОГРАММИСТ	PROGRAMMIST
PROGRAMMING	ПРОГРАММИРОВАНИЕ	PROGRAMMIROVANIYE
PROGRESS	ПРОГРЕСС	PROGRESS
PROGRESSION	ПРОГРЕССИЯ	PROGRESSIYA
PROJECT	ПРОЕКТ	PROYEKT
PROJECTION	ПРОЕКЦИЯ	PROYEKTSIYA
PROJECTOR	ПРОЕКТОР	PROYEKTOR

PROPAGANDA	ПРОПАГАНДА	PROPAGANDA
PROPOLIS	ПРОПОЛИС	PROPOLIS
PROPORTION	ПРОПОРЦИЯ	PROPORTSIYA
PROSTITUTE	ПРОСТИТУТКА	PROSTITUTKA
PROSTITUTION	ПРОСТИТУЦИЯ	PROSTITUTSIYA
PROSTRATION	ПРОСТРАЦИЯ	PROSTRATSIYA
PROTEST	ПРОТЕСТ	PROTEST
PROTOCOL	ПРОТОКОЛ	PROTOKOL
PROTOTYPE	ПРОТОТИП	PROTOTIP
PROVIDER	ПРОВАЙДЕР	PROVAYDER
PROVINCE	ПРОВИНЦИЯ	PROVINTSIYA
PSEUDONYM	ПСЕВДОНИМ	PSEVDONIM
PSYCHIATRY	ПСИХИАТРИЯ	PSIKHIATRIYA
PSYCHOLOGIST	ПСИХОЛОГ	PSIKHOLOG
PSYCHOLOGY	ПСИХОЛОГИЯ	PSIKHOLOGIYA
PSYCHOTHERAPY	ПСИХОТЕРАПИЯ	PSIKHOTERAPIYA
PUBLIC	ПУБЛИКА	PUBLIKA
PUBLICATION	ПУБЛИКАЦИЯ	PUBLIKATSIYA
PUBLICIST	ПУБЛИЦИСТ	PUBLITSIST
PUDDING	ПУДИНГ	PUDING
PULLOVER	ПУЛОВЕР	PULOVER
PULSE	ПУЛЬС	PUL'S

PUNCH	ПУНШ	PUNSH
PUNCTUATION	ПУНКТУАЦИЯ	PUNKTUATSIYA
PYRAMID	ПИРАМИДА	PIRAMIDA

Kick-start Learning Russian:
2000 RUSSIAN Words You didn't Know You Knew

Q

ENGLISH	RUSSIAN	PRONONSIATION
QUALIFICATION	КВАЛИФИКАЦИЯ	KVALIFIKATSIYA
QUARANTINE	КАРАНТИН	KARANTIN
QUARTET	КВАРТЕТ	KVARTET
QUARTZ	КВАРЦ	KVARTS
QUORUM	КВОРУМ	KVORUM
QUOTA	КВОТА	KVOTA

Kick-start Learning Russian:
2000 RUSSIAN Words You didn't Know You Knew

R

ENGLISH	RUSSIAN	PRONONSIATION
RACISM	РАСИЗМ	RASIZM
RACIST	РАСИСТ	RASIST
RADAR	РАДАР	RADAR
RADIATION	РАДИАЦИЯ	RADIATSIYA
RADICALISM	РАДИКАЛИЗМ	RADIKALIZM
RADIO	РАДИО	RADIO
RADIOACTIVITY	РАДИОАКТИВНОСТЬ	RADIOAKTIVNOST'
RADIOGRAM	РАДИОГРАММА	RADIOGRAMMA
RADIOTECHNICS	РАДИОТЕХНИКА	RADIOTEKHNIKA
RADIOTELEPHONE	РАДИОТЕЛЕФОН	RADIOTELEFON
RADIUS	РАДИУС	RADIUS
RADON	РАДОН	RADON
RALLY	РАЛЛИ	RALLI
RAPIER	РАПИРА	RAPIRA
RATIFICATION	РАТИФИКАЦИЯ	RATIFIKATSIYA
RATING	РЕЙТИНГ	REYTING
RATIONALISM	РАЦИОНАЛИЗМ	RATSIONALIZM

RATIONALIST	РАЦИОНАЛИСТ	RATSIONALIST
REACTION	РЕАКЦИЯ	REAKTSIYA
REACTOR	РЕАКТОР	REAKTOR
REALISM	РЕАЛИЗМ	REALIZM
REALIST	РЕАЛИСТ	REALIST
REBUS	РЕБУС	REBUS
RECONSTRUCTION	РЕКОНСТРУКЦИЯ	REKONSTRUKTSIYA
RECORD	РЕКОРД	REKORD
RECRUIT	РЕКРУТ	REKRUT
REEF	РИФ	RIF
REFEREE	РЕФЕРИ	REFERI
REFERENDUM	РЕФЕРЕНДУМ	REFERENDUM
REFLEX	РЕФЛЕКС	REFLEKS
REFORM	РЕФОРМА	REFORMA
REFRACTION	РЕФРАКЦИЯ	REFRAKTSIYA
REFRIGERATED	РЕФРИЖЕРАТОР	REFRIZHERATOR
REGATTA	РЕГАТА	REGATA
REGION	РАЙОН	RAYON
REGION	РЕГИОН	REGION
RELIEF	РЕЛЬЕФ	REL'YEF
RELIGION	РЕЛИГИЯ	RELIGIYA
REMARQUE	РЕМАРКА	REMARKA

RENT	РЕНТА	RENTA
REPERTOIRE	РЕПЕРТУАР	REPERTUAR
REPORT	РАПОРТ	RAPORT
REPORTAGE	РЕПОРТАЖ	REPORTAZH
REPRESSION	РЕПРЕССИЯ	REPRESSIYA
REPRISE	РЕПРИЗА	REPRIZA
REPRODUCTION	РЕПРОДУКЦИЯ	REPRODUKTSIYA
REPUBLIC	РЕСПУБЛИКА	RESPUBLIKA
REPUTATION	РЕПУТАЦИЯ	REPUTATSIYA
REQUIEM	РЕКВИЕМ	REKVIYEM
REQUISITE	РЕКВИЗИТ	REKVIZIT
RESERVE	РЕЗЕРВ	REZERV
RESERVOIR	РЕЗЕРВУАР	REZERVUAR
RESIDENT	РЕЗИДЕНТ	REZIDENT
RESONANCE	РЕЗОНАНС	REZONANS
RESOURCE	РЕСУРС	RESURS
RESPIRATOR	РЕСПИРАТОР	RESPIRATOR
RESTAURANT	РЕСТОРАН	RESTORAN
RESTORATION	РЕСТАВРАЦИЯ	RESTAVRATSIYA
RESULT	РЕЗУЛЬТАТ	REZUL'TAT
RESUME	РЕЗЮМЕ	REZYUME
RETRO	РЕТРО	RETRO
REVERENCE	РЕВЕРАНС	REVERANS

Kick-start Learning Russian:
2000 RUSSIAN Words You didn't Know You Knew

REVISION	РЕВИЗИЯ	REVIZIYA
REVOLUTION	РЕВОЛЮЦИЯ	REVOLYUTSIYA
REVOLVER	РЕВОЛЬВЕР	REVOL'VER
RHETORIC	РИТОРИКА	RITORIKA
RHYTHM	РИТМ	RITM
RICE	РИС	RIS
RICOCHET	РИКОШЕТ	RIKOSHET
RINGTONE	РИНГТОН	RINGTON
RISK	РИСК	RISK
RITUAL	РИТУАЛ	RITUAL
ROAMING	РОУМИНГ	ROUMING
ROBOT	РОБОТ	ROBOT
ROCKER	РОКЕР	ROKER
ROCKET	РАКЕТА	RAKETA
RODEO	РОДЕО	RODEO
ROMAN	РОМАН	ROMAN
ROMANCE	РОМАНС	ROMANS
ROMANTIC	РОМАНТИК	ROMANTIK
ROSE	РОЗА	ROZA
ROSEMARY	РОЗМАРИН	ROZMARIN
ROTOR	РОТОР	ROTOR
ROUTINE	РУТИНА	RUTINA

RUGBY РЕГБИ REGBI

Kick-start Learning Russian:
2000 RUSSIAN Words You didn't Know You Knew

S

ENGLISH	RUSSIAN	PRONONSIATION
SABOTAGE	САБОТАЖ	SABOTAZH
SADISM	САДИЗМ	SADIZM
SAFE	СЕЙФ	SEYF
SALAD	САЛАТ	SALAT
SALON	САЛОН	SALON
SALT	СОЛЬ	SOL'
SANCTION	САНКЦИЯ	SANKTSIYA
SANDALS	САНДАЛИИ	SANDALII
SANDWICH	САНДВИЧ	SANDVICH
SAPPHIRE	САПФИР	SAPFIR
SARCASM	САРКАЗМ	SARKAZM
SARCOPHAGUS	САРКОФАГ	SARKOFAG
SATELLITE	САТЕЛЛИТ	SATELLIT
SAUNA	САУНА	SAUNA
SAXOPHONE	САКСОФОН	SAKSOFON
SCALPEL	СКАЛЬПЕЛЬ	SKAL'PEL'
SCANDAL	СКАНДАЛ	SKANDAL

SCARF	ШАРФ	SHARF
SCENARIO	СЦЕНАРИЙ	STSENARIY
SCHNITZEL	ШНИЦЕЛЬ	SHNITSEL'
SEASON	СЕЗОН	SEZON
SECOND	СЕКУНДА	SEKUNDA
SECRET	СЕКРЕТ	SEKRET
SECRETAIRE	СЕКРЕТЕР	SEKRETER
SECTION	СЕКЦИЯ	SEKTSIYA
SECTOR	СЕКТОР	SEKTOR
SEISMOGRAPH	СЕЙСМОГРАФ	SEYSMOGRAF
SELECTION	СЕЛЕКЦИЯ	SELEKTSIYA
SELECTOR	СЕЛЕКТОР	SELEKTOR
SEMANTICS	СЕМАНТИКА	SEMANTIKA
SEMESTER	СЕМЕСТР	SEMESTR
SEMINAR	СЕМИНАР	SEMINAR
SENATE	СЕНАТ	SENAT
SENATOR	СЕНАТОР	SENATOR
SENSATION	СЕНСАЦИЯ	SENSATSIYA
SEPARATISM	СЕПАРАТИЗМ	SEPARATIZM
SEPARATOR	СЕПАРАТОР	SEPARATOR
SERVICE	СЕРВИС	SERVIS
SESSION	СЕССИЯ	SESSIYA

SEX	СЕКС	SEKS
SEX BOMB	СЕКС-БОМБА	SEKS-BOMBA
SEXOLOGY	СЕКСОЛОГИЯ	SEKSOLOGIYA
SHAMAN	ШАМАН	SHAMAN
SHAMPOO	ШАМПУНЬ	SHAMPUN'
SHARAD	ШАРАДА	SHARADA
SHARIAT	ШАРИАТ	SHARIAT
SHASHLYK	ШАШЛЫК	SHASHLYK
SHERIFF	ШЕРИФ	SHERIF
SHOCK	ШОК	SHOK
SHOPPING	ШОПИНГ	SHOPING
SHORT LIST	ШОРТ-ЛИСТ	SHORT-LIST
SHORTS	ШОРТЫ	SHORTY
SHOW	ШОУ	SHOU
SHOW BUSINESS	ШОУ-БИЗНЕС	SHOU-BIZNES
SHOWMAN	ШОУМЕН	SHOUMEN
SHOWROOM	ШОУРУМ	SHOURUM
SIGNAL	СИГНАЛ	SIGNAL
SIR	СЭР	SER
SISTER	СЕСТРА	SESTRA
SKEPTIC	СКЕПТИК	SKEPTIK
SKEPTICISM	СКЕПТИЦИЗМ	SKEPTITSIZM
SOCIOLOGIST	СОЦИОЛОГ	SOTSIOLOG

SOCIOLOGY	СОЦИОЛОГИЯ	SOTSIOLOGIYA
SON	СЫН	SYN
SOUP	СУП	SUP
SOUVENIR	СУВЕНИР	SUVENIR
SOVEREIGNTY	СУВЕРЕНИТЕТ	SUVERENITET
SPEECH	СПИЧ	SPICH
SPHERE	СФЕРА	SFERA
SPHINX	СФИНКС	SFINKS
SPONSOR	СПОНСОР	SPONSOR
SPORT	СПОРТ	SPORT
STABILIZATOR	СТАБИЛИЗАТОР	STABILIZATOR
STADIUM	СТАДИОН	STADION
STAMP	ШТАМП	SHTAMP
STAND	СТЕНД	STEND
STANDARD	СТАНДАРТ	STANDART
START	СТАРТ	START
STATE	ШТАТ	SHTAT
STATION	СТАНЦИЯ	STANTSIYA
STATISTICS	СТАТИСТИКА	STATISTIKA
STATUETTE	СТАТУЭТКА	STATUETKA
STATUS	СТАТУС	STATUS
STENOGRAPHY	СТЕНОГРАФИЯ	STENOGRAFIYA

STEREOTYPE	СТЕРЕОТИП	STEREOTIP
STETHOSCOPE	СТЕТОСКОП	STETOSKOP
STIMULATOR	СТИМУЛЯТОР	STIMULYATOR
STIMULUS	СТИМУЛ	STIMUL
STRATEGY	СТРАТЕГИЯ	STRATEGIYA
STRATOSPHERE	СТРАТОСФЕРА	STRATOSFERA
STRESS	СТРЕСС	STRESS
STRUCTURE	СТРУКТУРА	STRUKTURA
STUDIO	СТУДИЯ	STUDIYA
SUBSIDY	СУБСИДИЯ	SUBSIDIYA
SUBTROPICS	СУБТРОПИКИ	SUBTROPIKI
SUFFIX	СУФФИКС	SUFFIKS
SUPERMAN	СУПЕРМЕН	SUPERMEN
SUPINATOR	СУПИНАТОР	SUPINATOR
SURROGATE	СУРРОГАТ	SURROGAT
SYMBOL	СИМВОЛ	SIMVOL
SYMBOLOGY	СИМВОЛИКА	SIMVOLIKA
SYMMETRY	СИММЕТРИЯ	SIMMETRIYA
SYMPATHY	СИМПАТИЯ	SIMPATIYA
SYMPHONY	СИМФОНИЯ	SIMFONIYA
SYMPOSIUM	СИМПОЗИУМ	SIMPOZIUM
SYMPTOM	СИМПТОМ	SIMPTOM
SYNCHRONISM	СИНХРОНИЗМ	SINKHRONIZM

SYNCHRONIZER	СИНХРОНИЗАТОР	SINKHRONIZATOR
SYNDICATE	СИНДИКАТ	SINDIKAT
SYNDROME	СИНДРОМ	SINDROM
SYNONYM	СИНОНИМ	SINONIM
SYNTHESIS	СИНТЕЗ	SINTEZ
SYNTHETIC	СИНТЕТИКА	SINTETIKA
SYRUP	СИРОП	SIROP
SYSTEM	СИСТЕМА	SISTEMA
SYSTEMATICS	СИСТЕМАТИКА	SISTEMATIKA

T

ENGLISH	RUSSIAN	PRONONSIATION
TABLET	ТАБЛЕТКА	TABLETKA
TABOO	ТАБУ	TABU
TACTICS	ТАКТИКА	TAKTIKA
TALC	ТАЛЬК	TAL'K
TALENT	ТАЛАНТ	TALANT
TALK SHOW	ТОК-ШОУ	TOK-SHOU
TAMPON	ТАМПОН	TAMPON
TANGENT	ТАНГЕНС	TANGENS
TANK	ТАНК	TANK
TARIFF	ТАРИФ	TARIF
TAXI	ТАКСИ	TAKSI
TECHNICS	ТЕХНИКА	TEKHNIKA
TECHNOLOGIST	ТЕХНОЛОГ	TEKHNOLOG
TECHNOLOGY	ТЕХНОЛОГИЯ	TEKHNOLOGIYA
TELEFAX	ТЕЛЕФАКС	TELEFAKS
TELEGRAPH	ТЕЛЕГРАФ	TELEGRAF
TELEPATHY	ТЕЛЕПАТИЯ	TELEPATIYA

Kick-start Learning Russian:
2000 RUSSIAN Words You didn't Know You Knew

TELEPHONE	ТЕЛЕФОН	TELEFON
TELESCOPE	ТЕЛЕСКОП	TELESKOP
TELEVISION	ТЕЛЕВИЗОР	TELEVIZOR
TELEX	ТЕЛЕКС	TELEKS
TEMPERATURE	ТЕМПЕРАТУРА	TEMPERATURA
TEMPO	ТЕМП	TEMP
TENDENCY	ТЕНДЕНЦИЯ	TENDENTSIYA
TENOR	ТЕНОР	TENOR
TERMINAL	ТЕРМИНАЛ	TERMINAL
TERRACE	ТЕРРАСА	TERRASA
TERRARIUM	ТЕРРАРИУМ	TERRARIUM
TERRITORY	ТЕРРИТОРИЯ	TERRITORIYA
TERROR	ТЕРРОР	TERROR
TERRORISM	ТЕРРОРИЗМ	TERRORIZM
TERRORIST	ТЕРРОРИСТ	TERRORIST
TEST	ТЕСТ	TEST
TEXT	ТЕКСТ	TEKST
THEME	ТЕМА	TEMA
THEOREM	ТЕОРЕМА	TEOREMA
THEORY	ТЕОРИЯ	TEORIYA
THERAPY	ТЕРАПИЯ	TERAPIYA
THERMODYNAMICS	ТЕРМОДИНАМИКА	TERMODINAMIKA

THERMOS	ТЕРМОС	TERMOS
THERMOSTAT	ТЕРМОСТАТ	TERMOSTAT
THESIS	ТЕЗИС	TEZIS
THRILLER	ТРИЛЛЕР	TRILLER
THRONE	ТРОН	TRON
TIARA	ТИАРА	TIARA
TIGER	ТИГР	TIGR
TOAST	ТОСТ	TOST
TOASTER	ТОСТЕР	TOSTER
TOBACCO	ТАБАК	TABAK
TOILET	ТУАЛЕТ	TUALET
TOLERANCE	ТОЛЕРАНТНОСТЬ	TOLERANTNOST'
TOMATO	ТОМАТ	TOMAT
TON	ТОННА	TONNA
TONSILLITIS	ТОНЗИЛЛИТ	TONZILLIT
TOPOGRAPHY	ТОПОГРАФИЯ	TOPOGRAFIYA
TOREADOR	ТОРЕАДОР	TOREADOR
TOTALIZATOR	ТОТАЛИЗАТОР	TOTALIZATOR
TOUR	ТУР	TUR
TOURISM	ТУРИЗМ	TURIZM
TOURIST	ТУРИСТ	TURIST
TOXIN	ТОКСИН	TOKSIN
TRACHEA	ТРАХЕЯ	TRAKHEYA

TRACK	ТРЕК	TREK
TRACT	ТРАКТ	TRAKT
TRACTOR	ТРАКТОР	TRAKTOR
TRADING	ТРЕЙДИНГ	TREYDING
TRADITION	ТРАДИЦИЯ	TRADITSIYA
TRAFFIC	ТРАФИК	TRAFIK
TRAGEDY	ТРАГЕДИЯ	TRAGEDIYA
TRAINER	ТРЕНЕР	TRENER
TRAJECTORY	ТРАЕКТОРИЯ	TRAYEKTORIYA
TRANQUILIZER	ТРАНКВИЛИЗАТОР	TRANKVILIZATOR
TRANS	ТРАНС	TRANS
TRANSCRIPTION	ТРАНСКРИПЦИЯ	TRANSKRIPTSIYA
TRANSFER	ТРАНСФЕР	TRANSFER
TRANSFORMATION	ТРАНСФОРМАЦИЯ	TRANSFORMATSIYA
TRANSFORMER	ТРАНСФОРМАТОР	TRANSFORMATOR
TRANSISTOR	ТРАНЗИСТОР	TRANZISTOR
TRANSIT	ТРАНЗИТ	TRANZIT
TRANSLATION	ТРАНСЛЯЦИЯ	TRANSLYATSIYA
TRANSMISSION	ТРАНСМИССИЯ	TRANSMISSIYA
TRANSPLANTATION	ТРАНСПЛАНТАЦИЯ	TRANSPLANTATSIYA
TRANSPORT	ТРАНСПОРТ	TRANSPORT
TRANSPORTER	ТРАНСПОРТЁР	TRANSPORTOR

TRAPEZIUM	ТРАПЕЦИЯ	TRAPETSIYA
TRAUMA	ТРАВМА	TRAVMA
TRAUMATISM	ТРАВМАТИЗМ	TRAVMATIZM
TRAUMATOLOGY	ТРАВМАТОЛОГИЯ	TRAVMATOLOGIYA
TRAWLER	ТРАУЛЕР	TRAULER
TREND	ТРЕНД	TREND
TRIAD	ТРИАДА	TRIADA
TRIBUNAL	ТРИБУНАЛ	TRIBUNAL
TRIBUNE	ТРИБУНА	TRIBUNA
TRICK	ТРЮК	TRYUK
TRIGONOMETRY	ТРИГОНОМЕТРИЯ	TRIGONOMETRIYA
TRILOGY	ТРИЛОГИЯ	TRILOGIYA
TRIMMING	ТРИММИНГ	TRIMMING
TRIO	ТРИО	TRIO
TRIUMPH	ТРИУМФ	TRIUMF
TROPICS	ТРОПИКИ	TROPIKI
TSUNAMI	ЦУНАМИ	TSUNAMI
TUBE	ТЮБ	TYUB
TUBERCULOSIS	ТУБЕРКУЛЁЗ	TUBERKULOZ
TUNDRA	ТУНДРА	TUNDRA
TUNE	ТЮНИНГ	TYUNING
TUNNEL	ТОННЕЛЬ	TONNEL'
TURF	ТОРФ	TORF

Kick-start Learning Russian:
2000 RUSSIAN Words You didn't Know You Knew

TYPE	ТИП	TIP
TYPHOON	ТАЙФУН	TAYFUN
TYRANT	ТИРАН	TIRAN
TZAR	ЦАРЬ	TSAR'

U

ENGLISH	RUSSIAN	PRONONSIATION
UNBOXING	АНБОКСИНГ	ANBOKSING
UNIVERSAL	УНИВЕРСАЛ	UNIVERSAL
UNIVERSITY	УНИВЕРСИТЕТ	UNIVERSITET
UNLIMITED	АНЛИМИТЕД	ANLIMITED
UROLOGY	УРОЛОГИЯ	UROLOGIYA
UTOPIA	УТОПИЯ	UTOPIYA

V

ENGLISH	RUSSIAN	PRONONSIATION
VACANT	ВАКАНТНЫЙ	VAKANTNYY
VACCINE	ВАКЦИНА	VAKTSINA
VACUUM	ВАКУУМ	VAKUUM
VALERIAN	ВАЛЕРЬЯНА	VALER'YANA
VAMPIRE	ВАМПИР	VAMPIR
VANDALISM	ВАНДАЛИЗМ	VANDALIZM
VANILLIN	ВАНИЛИН	VANILIN
VASE	ВАЗА	VAZA
VASELINE	ВАЗЕЛИН	VAZELIN
VEGETARIAN	ВЕГЕТАРИАНЕЦ	VEGETARIANETS
VELOUR	ВЕЛЮР	VELYUR
VELVET	ВЕЛЬВЕТ	VEL'VET
VENDING	ВЕНДИНГ	VENDING
VERNISAGE	ВЕРНИСАЖ	VERNISAZH
VERSION	ВЕРСИЯ	VERSIYA
VIBRATOR	ВИБРАТОР	VIBRATOR
VICE-	ВИЦЕ-	VITSE-

VIDEO	ВИДЕО	VIDEO
VIRUS	ВИРУС	VIRUS
VISA	ВИЗА	VIZA
VISCOSE	ВИСКОЗА	VISKOZA
VISIT	ВИЗИТ	VIZIT
VITAMIN	ВИТАМИН	VITAMIN
VOLCANO	ВУЛКАН	VULKAN
VOLLEYBALL	ВОЛЕЙБОЛ	VOLEYBOL
VOLUNTEER	ВОЛОНТЁР	VOLONTIOR
VOUCHER	ВАУЧЕР	VAUCHER

W

ENGLISH	RUSSIAN	PRONONSIATION
WAFER	ВАФЛЯ	VAFLYA
WALTZ	ВАЛЬС	VAL'S
WATER	ВОДА	VODA
WATER POLO	ВАТЕРПОЛО	VATERPOLO
WEEKEND	УИКЕНД	UIKEND
WHISKY	ВИСКИ	VISKI

Kick-start Learning Russian:
2000 RUSSIAN Words You didn't Know You Knew

Y

ENGLISH	RUSSIAN	PRONONSIATION
YOGA	ЙОГА	Y**O**GA
YOGURT	ЙОГУРТ	Y**O**GURT

Z

ENGLISH	RUSSIAN	PRONONSIATION
ZOOLOGY	ЗООЛОГИЯ	ZOOL**O**GIYA

Kick-start Learning Russian:
2000 RUSSIAN Words You didn't Know You Knew

PICTURE QUIZ

Will you recognize Russian word?

1.

A. АККОРД

B. АВОКАДО

C. АКУСТИКА

D. АКРОБАТ

2.

A. КАКТУС

B. КОЛЛЕГА

C. КОЛЛЕДЖ

D. КОЛЛЕКЦИЯ

3.

A. ПОЭЗИЯ

B. ПОЛЮС

C. ПОРТРЕТ

D. ПОЛЕМИКА

4.

A. МУМИЯ

B. МОТОЦИКЛ

C. МУСС

D. МУНИЦИПАЛИТЕТ

5.

A. МЕХАНИК

B. МЕДИАНА

C. МЕДАЛЬ

D. МЕХАНИЗМ

6.

A. ТОСТ

B. ТИГР

C. ТАБАК

D. ТУАЛЕТ

7.

A. ГАЛАКТИКА

B. ГЕОМЕТРИЯ

C. ГЛАДИАТОР

D. ГЛИЦЕРИН

8.

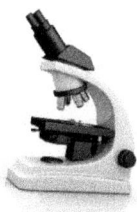

A. МУЗЫКА

B. МУЗЕЙ

C. МУСКУЛ

D. МИКРОСКОП

9.

A. ПИЖАМА

B. ПУБЛИЦИСТ

C. ПУДИНГ

D. ПУЛОВЕР

10.

A.   ДРАМА

B.   ДРАКОН

C.   ДРЕСС-КОД

D.   ДРЕЙФ

11.

A.   МОНИТОР

B.   МОЛЛЮСК

C.   МОНОГРАФИЯ

D.   МОЛЕКУЛА

12.

A.   ПИПЕТКА

B.   ПИЛОТ

C.   ПИОНЕР

D.   ПИАНИНО

QUESTION QUIZ

1. A small appliance designed to toast multiple types of bread products is called

    A. ТОМАТ
    B. ТОСТЕР
    C. ТАБАК
    D. ТУАЛЕТ

2. The study of past events, particularly in human affairs is called

    A. ХОББИ
    B. ГИППОПОТАМ
    C. ИСТОРИЯ
    D. ХОККЕЙ

3. A personal hygiene product designed to control sweating and body odour is called

    A. ДЕЗОДОРАНТ
    B. ДЕПОЗИТ
    C. ДЕРМАТОЛОГ
    D. ДЕПРЕССИЯ

4. A platform or compartment housed in a shaft for raising and lowering people or things to different levels is called

    A. ЛОТЕРЕЯ
    B. ЛИФТ
    C. ЛИМОНАД
    D. ЛОГИКА

5. An official representing a country abroad is called

    A.   ДЕФЕКТ

    B.   ДЕКОРАТОР

    C.   ДЕФИЦИТ

    D.   ДИПЛОМАТ

6. A cloth canopy which fills with air and allows a person or heavy object attached to it to descend slowly when dropped from an aircraft is called

    A.   ПАРАШЮТ

    B.   ПОЛИГЛОТ

    C.   ПРЕСТИЖ

    D.   ПРЕЗИДЕНТ

7. A polite expression of praise or admiration is called

    A.   КЛИМАТ

    B.   КЛОУН

    C.   КОМПЛИМЕНТ

    D.   КЛУБ

8. A place where aircraft take off and land, usually equipped with hard-surfaced landing strips, a control tower, hangars, aircraft maintenance and refueling facilities, and accommodations for passengers and cargo is called

    A.   АЭРОПОРТ

    B.   АССИСТЕНТ

    C.   АРОМАТ

    D.   АСБЕСТ

9. A line notionally drawn on the earth equidistant from the poles, dividing the earth into northern and southern hemispheres and constituting the parallel of latitude 0° is called

    A. ЭНЕРГИЯ
    B. ЭКВАТОР
    C. ЭНТУЗИАЗМ
    D. ИНЖЕНЕР

10. The rubbing and kneading of muscles and joints of the body with the hands, especially to relieve tension or pain is called

    A. МАТАДОР
    B. МАТЕРИАЛ
    C. МАСТИКА
    D. МАССАЖ

11. A bullfighter whose task is to kill the bull is called

    A. МАТАДОР
    B. МАТЕРИАЛ
    C. МАСТИКА
    D. МАССАЖ

12. A man or boy in relation to other sons and daughters of his parents is called

    A. БРАТ
    B. БРОНХИТ
    C. БРИФИНГ
    D. БРИЗ

Kick-start Learning Russian:
2000 RUSSIAN Words You didn't Know You Knew

SPORT PICTURE QUIZ

1.

    A.   АССИСТЕНТ

    B.   АКРОБАТ

    C.   МОНУМЕНТ

    D.   АВИАЦИЯ

2.

    A.   ФУТБОЛ

    B.   ФОРМАТ

    C.   ФОРМАЛИСТ

    D.   ФИРМА

3.

    A.   ТЕХНИКА

    B.   ТЕННИС

    C.   ТАКСИ

    D.   ТАРИФ

4.

A.   БАСКЕТБОЛ

B.   БАНДИТ

C.   БАНАН

D.   БАНК

5.

A.   ГАДЖЕТ

B.   ГАЛАКТИКА

C.   ГИМНАСТ

D.   ГИРЛЯНДА

6.

A.   ГРАФИКА

B.   ГОЛЬФ

C.   ГИТАРА

D.   ГРУППА

7.

A. ВОЛЕЙБОЛ

B. ВАМПИР

C. ВАНДАЛИЗМ

D. ВАЗЕЛИН

8.

A. БУФЕТ

B. БУЛЬДОГ

C. БАМПЕР

D. БОКС

9.

A. БАЛАНС

B. БЕЙСБОЛ

C. БАЛКОН

D. БАЛЛАДА

10.

A. БАДМИНТОН

B. БАРМЕН

C. БАРОМЕТР

D. БАРРИКАДА

11.

A. МАНЕКЕН

B. МАНСАРДА

C. МАНТИЯ

D. МАРАФОН

12.

A. СЕРФИНГ

B. СЕКУНДА

C. СЕКРЕТ

D. СЕКРЕТЕР

PROFESSIONS PICTURE QUIZ

1.

A. ДЖЕМ

B. ДЖИНСЫ

C. ДАНТИСТ

D. ДЖЕМПЕР

2.

A. ДЖУНГЛИ

B. ДОКТОР

C. ДЗЮДО

D. ДЖИП

3.

A. ВЕТЕРИНАР

B. ВАКЦИНА

C. ВАМПИР

D. ВАНИЛИН

4.

A. ФОРМАЛИЗМ

B. ФОРМУЛА

C. ФОРУМ

D. ФАРМАЦЕВТ

5.

A. АРХИТЕКТОР

B. АЭРОДИНАМИКА

C. АГРЕССИЯ

D. АЭРОПОРТ

6.

A. СКАНДАЛ

B. СТЮАРДЕССА

C. СКАЛЬПЕЛЬ

D. СЦЕНАРИЙ

7.

A. ФОРМАЛИСТ

B. ФОРТУНА

C. ФОТОГРАФ

D. ФОРМАТ

8.

A. СЕКРЕТАРЬ

B. СЕКУНДА

C. СЕКЦИЯ

D. СЕЗОН

9.

A. ПАРАШЮТ

B. ПАРАДОКС

C. ПИЛОТ

D. ПАНОРАМА

10.

A.   БРОНХИТ

B.   БОЙКОТ

C.   БРИФИНГ

D.   БАРМЕН

11.

A.   ФЕМИНИСТ

B.   ФЕРМЕР

C.   ФАВОРИТ

D.   ФАТАЛИСТ

12.

A.   ЭЛЕКТРИК

B.   ЭСКАЛАТОР

C.   ЭСКИМО

D.   ЭСПЕРАНТО

QUIZES ANSWERS

PICTURE QUIZ ANSWERS

1. **B**. АВОКАДО
2. **A**. КАКТУС
3. **C**. ПОРТРЕТ
4. **B**. МОТОЦИКЛ
5. **C**. МЕДАЛЬ
6. **A**. ТОСТ
7. **C**. ГЛАДИАТОР
8. **D**. МИКРОСКОП
9. **A**. ПИЖАМА
10. **B**. ДРАКОН
11. **A**. МОНИТОР
12. **D**. ПИАНИНО

QUESTION QUIZ ANSWERS

1. **B**. ТОСТЕР
2. **C**. ИСТОРИЯ
3. **A**. ДЕЗОДОРАНТ
4. **B**. ЛИФТ
5. **D**. ДИПЛОМАТ
6. **A**. ПАРАШЮТ
7. **C**. КОМПЛИМЕНТ
8. **A**. АЭРОПОРТ
9. **B**. ЭКВАТОР
10. **D**. МАССАЖ
11. **A**. МАТАДОР
12. **A**. БРАТ

SPORT PICTURE QUIZ ANSWERS

1. **B**. АКРОБАТ
2. **A**. ФУТБОЛ
3. **B**. ТЕННИС
4. **A**. БАСКЕТБОЛ
5. **C**. ГИМНАСТ
6. **B**. ГОЛЬФ
7. **A**. ВОЛЕЙБОЛ
8. **D**. БОКС
9. **B**. БЕЙСБОЛ
10. **A**. БАДМИНТОН
11. **D**. МАРАФОН
12. **A**. СЕРФИНГ

PROFESSIONS PICTURE QUIZ ANSWERS

1. **C**. ДАНТИСТ
2. **B**. ДОКТОР
3. **A**. ВЕТЕРИНАР
4. **D**. ФАРМАЦЕВТ
5. **A**. АРХИТЕКТОР
6. **B**. СТЮАРДЕССА
7. **C**. ФОТОГРАФ
8. **A**. СЕКРЕТАРЬ
9. **C**. ПИЛОТ
10. **D**. БАРМЕН
11. **B**. ФЕРМЕР
12. **A**. ЭЛЕКТРИК

ABOUT THE AUTHOR

Lawrence is a language enthusiast. In his spare time, he likes to read and learn new languages. He knows how to live on a manageable budget to have enough money to travel the world. He learned Russian because he wanted to communicate with ordinary people while traveling to the world's oldest and deepest freshwater Lake Baikal located in Russian Siberia and at The Summer Palace, a residence of Peter the Great in St.Petersburg.

FROM THE AUTHOR

Russian is not an easy language to learn. I put together this book as I was truly excited to let you know that there are 2000 RUSSIAN Words You didn't Know You Knew. There has never been a published dictionary like this. I hope you like the book.

If you enjoyed this book or if you found it helpful please take a moment post a positive review on the book's Amazon Page. You will notice a button that says "Write a customer review" - Just click on it and you're all set.

Thanks for your support!

You may also like to check out my books "Russian Words You didn't Know You Knew: Food Edition" and "TIME to WAKE UP: SAVE MONEY and GET OUT of DEBT" published at Amazon Kindle.

– Lawrence

NOTES

Lawrence Burns